THE GREAT FOREST
An Appalachian Story

Cover photograph by Gretchen Whisnant

THE GREAT FOREST
An Appalachian Story

Barry M. Buxton *editor*

Sam Gray *editor, 2nd edition*

This publication has been produced in consultation with the Museums Committee of the Appalachian Consortium and was supported by grants from the National Endowment for the Humanities and the North Carolina Department of Cultural Resourses.

The Appalachian Consortium was a non-profit educational organization composed of institutions and agencies located in Southern Appalachia. From 1973 to 2004, its members published pioneering works in Appalachian studies documenting the history and cultural heritage of the region. The Appalachian Consortium Press was the first publisher devoted solely to the region and many of the works it published remain seminal in the field to this day.

With funding from the Andrew W. Mellon Foundation and the National Endowment for the Humanities through the Humanities Open Book Program, Appalachian State University has published new paperback and open access digital editions of works from the Appalachian Consortium Press.

www.collections.library.appstate.edu/appconsortiumbooks

ISBN (pbk.: alk. Paper): 978-1-4696-3843-0
ISBN (ebook): 978-1-4696-3845-4

Distributed by the University of North Carolina Press
www.uncpress.org

TABLE OF CONTENTS

INTRODUCTION

Until recent time a great, almost unbroken, forest overlay the eastern portion of North America. This forest has its origins in an ancient circumpolar forest system that was here on earth when the continents of the Northern hemisphere were joined into one land mass, millions of years ago. When the continents separated and began their slow geologic drift, this ancient forest migrated into the middle latitudes of Asia, Europe, and North America. This migration and biological differentiation was later quickened and channeled by successive glacial epochs beginning 50,000 years ago and ending, in geologic time, only yesterday.

Thus the forest of Eastern North America is at once very ancient and very young. It is botannically linked to existing forest remnants in Europe, central Asia, and Japan. It was, until recently, a continuous biologic fabric extending from Nova Scotia to Alabama and westward along tributaries of the Mississippi. It is characterized by an extraordinary variety of plant, animal, and human communities. It is geophysically dominated by the long spine of the Appalachian mountains that determine its diversity and structure. It has been variously described as "Eastern Hardwood," deciduous, tropophytic, cool-temperate, and Appalachian.

For purposes of this essay and exhibition, acknowledging its breadth of range, extent of history, its immense productive capacity and diversity, and its power to affect human society and spirit, it will be referred to as THE GREAT FOREST.

Of all its myriad populations, none have so changed the Great Forest as the humans. From the time of their arrival at the end of the last glacial epoch (10,000 B.C.), using, at first, technologies of stone, fire, fibre, and wood, the earliest people affected and were themselves affected by the forest. This technological and cultural dialectic of human and wilderness continued with increased intensity until the present, when, with so many of the former and so little of the latter, the process threatens to collapse in imbalance.

During the late 19th and 20th century, industrial interests exploited most heavily the natural resources of the western and southern portions of the Great Forest. The environmental impact was so great that we used it as a yardstick to judge other uses of the forest in other times. By this measure, pre-industrial use of the forest seems minimal; neither the white settler nor the Indian would seem to have made much impact on his environment. This assumption, however, ignores the very delicate nature of the eco-system which is affected by *any* human participation.

William Cronon's ecological history of New England, *Changes in the Land: Indians, Colonists, and the Ecology of New England,* documents the profound ecological impact of early white settlements in this northern region of the forest. Cronon's point is not that the Indian had little impact on his environment, but that the nature of his impact differed from that of the Europeans. "The choice is not between two landscapes, one with and one without a human influence; it is between two human ways of living, two ways of belonging to an ecosystem." The difference in impact was due not only to different uses of the environments, but to different attitudes about its resources.

The history of the forest then is, in part, a history of the changing meanings man has ascribed to the forest. Few people of the most distant past left artifacts from which we can clearly read this meaning. Their artifacts often tell us how they *used* the forest, but not what they thought of it. We know nothing of the myths and stories the ancient people told in order to comprehend their place in the green, living world that extended endlessly on all sides. The fact that it was their home and home to all the creatures and plants they depended on would doubtless imbue the forest with many levels of meaning, but these levels are inaccessible to us now.

Still, the study of the *use* of the forest and the technology developed to achieve this use is an appropriate way to understand the forest's cultural meaning. Under stable cultural conditions, humans are guided in their use of the environment by the values they place upon it. The cultural meaning of the forest, however, should not be read solely by the extent of the culture's ability to modify the environment. Similar levels of technology do not necessarily mean similar value systems just as radically different levels of technology may obscure similar values. Anne Rogers, in the first of four essays that follow, orders and interprets the archeological record in an effort to understand prehistoric cultures in the context of the Forest.

An ecological history of the southern Appalachian forest might reveal equally profound differences between the *impact* of Indian and white systems of forest resource use. Cronon argues that the Europeans' "perception of 'resources' were filtered through the language of 'commodities.' " To what extent the white settlers of the Southern Appalachians regarded the forest that surrounded them as a commodity is subject to debate. While the white colonists of New England and the settlers of Southern Appalachia broadly shared the same culture, the economic climates of the two regions were quite different. The difficulty of transportation in and out of the mountains made it difficult for the Appalachian to market the resources of the forest, except at the local level. One might even argue that there was a reluctance to treat natural resources as commodities among a segment of the rural Appalachian society. The long survival of log building technology in the region is attributable, in part, to the willingness of rural people to participate in cooperative labor exchange and build with timber in a relatively unrefined state, rather than participate in the cash economy by purchasing building materials. The long continuation of the free range system may also be seen as a resistance to treating forest lands as a commodity, as it stresses cooperative use rather than private ownership of forest lands. Finally, in the case of at least one significant usage pattern, that of hunting, the 19th century Southern Appalachian was probably closer in attitude to prehistoric hunter/gatherers than to his own contemporaries in the already decimated and industrialized northern regions of the original forest. Tyler Blethen and Curtis Wood trace these and related issues of the settlement period in the second essay of this volume.

If the white settler of the southern Appalachian mountains did not actively perceive forest resources as commodities, his view of those resources was ultimately of a utilitarian nature. This attitude, which was supported by his religion and worldview, emphasized the domination of nature by man. It is this idea that most differentiates white from prehistoric attitudes. Although his technological means were limited, the settler brought what he could of his environment under his control. Perhaps it is for this reason that when the railroad enabled the industrial exploitation of the forest, Appalachians generally accepted and cooperated in this industrial use, though the impetus for it came from outside their society. They accepted the value of exploiting the forest for practical purposes, though they could not predict the impact to the forests or their own lifestyes nor the fact that they, as well as the forest, would be treated as resources by industry. Ron Eller's essay on the use and misuse of forest resource and people broadens our understanding of this period.

It is noteworthy that, despite the negative environmental, social, and economic affects of the industrial use of the forest, many rural Appalachians later aligned themselves even more emphatically with industrial interests in perceiving alternate uses of the forest, inspired by romantic, ecological, or preservational attitudes, as the ultimate threat. The establishment of the first school of Forestry near Brevard, N. C.

The dominant ethic of the industrial era timber harvesters, whether big operator or small, was to haul away as much of the forest as fast as possible.

and the subsequent development of scientific forestry offered an alternative way of using the forest from that of the destruction of the industrial era in Southern Appalachia. The goals of scientific forestry, however, were ultimately utilitarian in nature, and it would eventually become an ally and not an enemy of industry, although its proponents advocated modification of the *methods* of industrial use of the forest. From the early 1930's to the present, industry has felt more threatened by those who perceive the forest by aesthetic, ecologic, or romantic criteria and thereby advocate preservation and conservation of the remains of the forest.

By the late 19th century many non-Appalachian parts of the Eastern United States were feeling the effects of the disappearance of wilder places from their landscape. This disappearance encouraged romantic attitudes toward wilderness and fueled a movement to preserve those areas of wilderness which survived. The movement to create a national park in the East, which focused on the Great Smoky Mountains, pitted these romantic notions of wilderness against the local rural population. (Those local interests who prompted the establishment of the park also had utilitarian motives, as they saw tourism as ultimately a more profitable industry than forestry.)

Part of the conflict over the establishment of the park arose over the differing perceptions of whether the area was a wilderness. One industry, which initially opposed the creation of the park, took out a full page advertisement in the *Asheville Citizen* to discuss the issue. They advocated that the area be placed under the jurisdiction of the Forest Service to be managed under the principles of scientific forestry, rather than be turned over to the National Park Service. "These are not undeveloped and wild lands," they argued, the land having already been modified for industrial use.

For the approximatley one-thousand families who lived within the proposed boundaries of the park, the area was also not a wilderness, it was a home. Although some sold out willingly, the forced removal of some families left a legacy of bitterness towards federal intervention.

More recent efforts to establish alternate uses of the Appalachian forest have been guided by ecological attitudes. Again, the conflicts which arise focus not just on how the forest should be used, but also on why it should be used in various ways. In recent history we have seen the repeated conflicts between whether what remains of the forest should be under private ownership (and utilized in whatever way the owner sees fit) or whether the government should control use. Even within federal management, the long standing conflict between ulititarian and idealistic attitudes toward use of natural resources (a conflict which has its roots in the very beginning of the conservation movement) continues to be an issue in the formation of policy. The last essay by Harley Jolley deals with aspects of federal involvement in forest conservation, particulary through agencies such as the CCC and Job Corps.

In the headlines of local papers, we see evidence of the continuing conflict between values and attitudes of the forest. It is not always easy to ascribe a consistant set of values to any segment of the forest's users. In a modern pluralistic society, ideas and attitudes move swiftly through different constituencies. Where once many rural people defended their right to use the forest for utilitarian purposes against federal intervention on behalf of those who would preserve the forest for aesthetic reasons, some now criticize the government on aesthetic grounds for its utilitarian use of the forest (such as the Forest Service's clear cutting policy). To appease the various interests, the remnants of the forest have been carved into pieces designated for different purposes, and the debate goes on.

In examining the meanings of the forest, we realize that the Appalachian forest is not just a natural landscape, it is a cultural landscape. Man has drastically modified its physical structure and, in the process, infused it with successive cultural meanings. Attempts to preserve what is left of the forest in its "natural" state is a reflection of the most recent of these meanings—the meaning we find in wilderness itself. In studying the Appalachian forest, we learn about ourselves and our ever more complex relationship to the forest.

Sam Gray
Greasy Creek

Michael Ann Williams
University of Illinois

THE GREAT FOREST: PREHISTORY

The Southern Appalachian woodlands have been important to humans ever since the earliest inhabitants of this area arrived here. Even though no one knows exactly when this area was first occupied, it is not difficult to imagine the rugged beauty of the forested mountains when the first people came here. The clear, fast-flowing streams, the towering trees, and panoramic views from the high peaks must have been as impressive then as they are today.

Much of what we know about these native inhabitants has been learned through archaeological interpretation. Archaeologists, using scientific methods, can determine such things as the kinds of animals hunted and the types of vegetable foods gathered; the places where stone for making tools was obtained; the ways prehistoric people moved from place to place to use different resources at different times during the year; as well as much more. Since prehistoric people left no written records of their activities, it is mainly through archaeological research that we obtain information about past lifeways.

Archaeologists also use historic accounts written by early travelers and traders in reconstructing the past. These people sometimes wrote about the native inhabitants they encountered, and often their accounts provide the only record of the American Indian groups which were occupying the southern Appalachian woodlands when Europeans first came here. While some aspects of prehistoric life can never be retrieved, the combination of archaeological research with historic information does make possible a fairly comprehensive interpretation of the ways in which prehistoric peoples lived.

The prehistory of the southern Appalachian area follows the same archaeological sequence generally recognized for all of Eastern North America. The major prehistoric periods defined by archaeologists are Paleo-Indian, Archaic, and Woodland, followed in some areas by the Mississippian period. Each of these has been defined on the basis of technology, settlement patterns, and food procurement practices.

The earliest of these, the Paleo-Indian, is known in the southern Appalachian area only from isolated surface occurrences of fluted spear points. It is thought that during this time, small nomadic groups of people hunted and gathered their food by moving from place to place, staying for only brief periods of time in any one location. Large game animals are thought to have been their main source of protein food. This period began around, 12,000 B.C., or perhaps earlier, and lasted until around 8000 B.C.

The succeeding period, the Archaic, is characterized by changes in subsistence practices and settlement patterns. The beginning of the Archaic period coincided with the warmer climate associated with the northward retreat of the glaciers which had previously covered portions of what is now the United States. It was at this time that weather conditions similar to those of the present time were established. Large mammals such as mammoths and mastodons became extinct, and it was necessary for the prehistoric occupants of the area to rely on deer and small game for their animal protein requirements. This change in climate was also accompanied by changes in vegetation. One of the most important changes was an increase in the number of nut-producing trees. These and other deciduous trees replaced many of the evergreens which were the main forest cover during times when the climate was colder.

The Archaic period lasted for about 7,000 years. During that time, lifestyles continued to be nomadic, but there is evidence for increased specialization in the manufacture of tools and utensils used for processing vegetable foods. Fishing and shellfish collecting also became important at this time. Nuts were used as sources of vegetable protein and fat.

By around 1000 B.C., there is evidence for the development of a relatively settled mode of existence throughout the Eastern United States. This period, known as the Woodland, lasted until around A.D. 800 in many areas of the Southern Appalachians, and until the time of European contact in others. During this time, there is good evidence for the intentional planting of food crops, at least on a small scale, and for the development of settled village life.

There also appear at this time indications of extensive trade in items such as marine shell from the Gulf of Mexico, copper from the Great Lakes and other regions, and mica from the southern Appalachian mountains. These materials were used in ritual contexts, and artifacts made from them are frequently found associated with burials of important individuals who were often interred in mounds constructed for that purpose.

Extensive trade and the construction of burial mounds indicate a decrease in the amount of labor needed to obtain food, resulting in an increase of the amount of time available for other purposes. Pottery vessels began to be manufactured early in the Woodland period. These were used for both cooking and storage, and were sometimes decorated

2

Cherokee using blow gun. (pen and ink drawing by Sandy Lidh based on material from Museum of the Cherokee Indian)

with distinctive designs. Decorative motifs were also engraved on shell. Items of personal adornment may have indicated differences in status. Bows and arrows replaced spears as weapons for killing game.

In the southernmost part of the Appalachian area, the Woodland period was succeeded by the Mississippian. This period was characterized by increased reliance on domesticated plants for food and by the construction of larger pyramid-shaped mounds. These mounds served

3

as bases for the structures used by the leaders of the village for both religious and political functions.

The early European explorers who visited this area described the native inhabitants as farmers who lived in houses constructed by covering the sides of wooden framework with clay and then roofing the structure with bark shingles. In their gardens, they cultivated a number of plants, including corn, beans, and squash. They also continued to gather many wild plants for food and for medicinal use. Their only domesticated animal was the dog, and they relied on hunting and fishing to obtain animal protein foods.

By the mid-1600's the influence of European contact to the east and north began to be felt throughout the southern Appalachian woodlands. Later, the area was visited by both explorers and traders, and eventually was settled by non-Indians during the period of western expansion into this part of the continent. Initially, most of these non-Indians were traders, but by the early 1800's families had begun to move into the area. Finally, in the late 1830's, the removal of most of the Indian populations was effected, and only a fraction of the people who had formerly occupied the southern Appalachian woodlands remained behind in their homeland.

These original inhabitants of the areas considered themselves to be participants in the natural world which surrounded them rather than manipulators of their environment. The forests and the resources which they contained were there for their use, belonging not to individuals but to all who needed those things which could be found there.

Almost all of life's basic necessities were available in the woodlands. Food and clothing were provided by the animals which lived in the forest. Shelters were constructed from tree trunks, bark, and vines. Numerous plants provided both food and medicine. Streams that ran through the forests were sources of water for drinking and bathing. Even the materials used for making stone tools of various types were found there.

Although some domesticated plants were cultivated in later times, the woodlands continued to supply much of the plant food and almost all of the animal food necessary to sustain life. If one had the requisite knowledge, it was possible to find every necessary dietary component. In fact, forests continued to be important sources of animal protein even into historic times.

The most important animal was the deer. According to one report, in the year 1844, the Indians living in Quallatown, near present-day Cherokee, killed 540 deer. They also killed 78 bears in that same year. Birds, small mammals, fish, and amphibians such as turtles would have supplemented these large-body animals as sources of protein.

Although bears were killed in fewer numbers than deer, no doubt because of their lesser frequency in the wild, they were particularly important because of the fat they provided. This fat was used not only for food but was used to soften leather, as a hair dressing, and for a multitude of other purposes.

The forest also supplied fat and protein in another form. Methods for extracting oils from nuts are known to have been practiced by American Indians in the early historic period, and it is probable that these same methods had been in use for hundreds, and perhaps thousands, of years.

The main source of vegetable oil was the hickory nut. Charred remains of hickory shells have been recovered from archaeological sites dating as far back as 4000 B.C. Several observers commented on the use of oil extracted from hickory nuts by historic Indian groups. Among them was William Bartram, a naturalist who traveled through the southern Appalachian area in the 1770's. He noted that the oil was extracted from the nuts by crushing the nuts, boiling them in water, and then retrieving the fat which rose to the surface. Bartram observed that some families had as much as 100 pounds of hickory oil stored in their houses.

The use of hickory nuts by some Cherokee Indians has extended into the present time. A dish called hickory nut soup is made by pounding the nuts, removing as much of the shell as possible, and cooking the nut meat in boiling water. The shell which remains settles to the bottom. Sometimes nuts prepared this way are used to thicken meat broths and may also be used to prepare a beverage.

Before the disappearance of native chestnuts from southern Appalachian forests, these nuts were used in the preparation of a dish called "chestnut bread." It is still prepared by modern Cherokees using Chinese chestnuts. Chestnuts are combined with corn meal; the mixture is formed into balls, wrapped in hickory leaves, and boiled.

Other nuts were important as well but not to the extent that the hickory nuts and chestnuts were. Even acorns can be edible if processed properly, but they are not likely to have been a preferred food if other types of nuts were available.

Among the trees which provided kinds of food other than nuts were persimmons and honey locusts. Persimmons were not only eaten as a fruit but were combined with corn meal to make persimmon bread; the honey locust pods were boiled to make a sweet tasting drink.

Seeds and berries were also collected from plants growing in the forest. Blueberries, buckberries, and blackberries were among the fruits available, and seeds of such plants as amaranth, sunflowers, and smart grass were eaten as well.

The number of gathered plants still used by many Cherokees reflects their importance in the past. In addition to nuts and plants already mentioned, leaves and stems of the coneflower (Rudbeckia laciniata L.) called "sochan" by the Cherokees, are cooked as a green vegetable. Leaves of a number of other wild plants are used in a similar manner.

Several varieties of mushrooms and other fungi are still gathered. These are considered delicacies by the Cherokees. Ramps, onion-like plants, are gathered in the spring and eaten both raw and cooked.

Some plants were used for medicinal purposes, as was the bark of certain trees. A Cherokee formula for treating a children's disease known as "something is causing something to eat," referring to stomach pain in infants, required that the patient be bathed in water in which the barks of sassafras, flowering dogwood, service, and black gum trees had been steeped. The cure for chills and fever involved blowing water in which wild cherry bark had been steeped over the body of the patient. An infusion of wild cherry bark was also used in the treatment of a disease called "yellow," which was characterized by jaundice-like symptoms.

Although little information is available about the ritual uses or special properties of various types of wood, the Cherokees divided trees into evergreen and deciduous categories. Among the evergreens, cedar was attributed special status. The wood of cedar trees was not used for fuel, but small twigs were sometimes placed on the fire during ceremonies.

The houses of southeastern Indians during early historic times were both sturdy and substantial. They were intended to be permanent structures rather than temporary shelters, and the materials used in their construction were no doubt carefully chosen to be durable.

There is archaeological evidence to indicate that the type of construction observed by early travelers in the area was not a recent innovation. Houses of at least a semi-permanent nature may have been constructed as early as 2000 B.C. Later in time, larger structures used for political and ceremonial purposes may have used as many as 150 posts three to four inches in diameter in their construction. Some of the later villages also were surrounded by palisades, possibly for protection. Sometimes the areas around the mounds in larger villages were also set off by palisades.

Transportation in the southern Appalachian woodlands was either overland by foot trails or by river. For river travel, canoes were constructed from large trees hollowed out first by burning and finished with woodworking tools made from stone. The importance of selecting the proper type of wood for this purpose is indicated by the fact that

Cherokee women fashioning a basket from white oak. Dark splints were dyed with black walnut root. Onconaluftee Indian Village.

A Cherokee water drum. Often of sycamore, these drums were partially filled with water to affect the tone

the Cherokee word for canoe, "tsi:yu," is the same as the word for poplar tree.

Wood was also used for a number of other items important to the inhabitants of the Southern Appalachians. The mortars and pestles used by the women for pounding corn were made from wood. Wooden bowls were used for serving food. Roots of the butternut tree were used for making a dark dye, and roots of bloodroot plants, found in the forest, were used to make a red-orange dye.

Baskets were made from a variety of materials, among them wood and bark. Wooden baskets were made from white oak split into thin strips and woven into various shapes. Baskets were also made from

7

vines and peeled river cane. Not only did these containers serve as utilitarian items, but they were also the vehicle for artistic expression. Dyed vines or strips of wood or cane were combined to create intricate patterns in the bodies of many containers.

The long term use of wood by the native inhabitants of the southern Appalachian forest is indicated by the addition of stone tools used for cutting and working wood into prehistoric tool kits by around 3000 B.C. Although ground stone is not as desirable as metal for making tools for woodworking, it can be resharpened to renew the edge.

That the woodlands were essential to the survival of the prehistoric occupants of the Southern Appalachians is clear. The woodlands were central to every aspect of their lives, providing food, shelter and clothing. It is unlikely that modern inhabitants of this area will ever appreciate fully the importance of woodland resources to these people. However, study of the past through archaeology can at least expand our understanding of the potential for supporting human life inherent in the forests and enhance our appreciation for resources which they contain.

Anne Rogers
Western Carolina University

A PROCESS BEGUN: THE SETTLEMENT ERA

The human effort to tame and use the woodland is a constant theme in history. At times when vast areas of the world were covered with woods, utilization of the forest meant survival. In more recent ages, it has meant wealth. Success in either case lay in finding means to clear forest land for agriculture or for animals and ways to use trees and their by-products for human benefit. Often the forest reasserted itself and grew back, but the net result, over time, has been ever more open space at the expense of woodland.

The earliest white settlers to confront the southern Appalachian forest lands were Europeans. The great majority came from the British Isles, but significant numbers came from central Europe. When they came to America they brought with them a whole set of attitudes, skills, and expectations, some more appropriate than others, which influenced their interaction with the mountain forests. In order to understand their response to the American woodland, it is first necessary to understand their European experience.

At the dawn of prehistory, western and central Europe was covered with a heavy mantle of woods broken only where the Alps and the Carpathian Mountains rose above the tree line and where the soil was too marshy to support trees. It was a deciduous growth, predominantly oak but mixed with elm, beech, linden, and hazel.

In the pre-agricultural era man lived beneath its canopy much like the American Indian, hunting its wildlife, gathering its fruits and berries, using its branches for fuel and its trunks for crude boats. With the invention of agriculture, man for the first time began hesitantly to clear the land with axe and fire. But it was a primative beginning, for tools were simple and areas with heavy clay soils remained immune until the invention of the heavy plow made it possible to break up such ground.

Some clearing of land occurred in western and central Europe during its occupation by the Romans, but only with the fall of the Roman Empire and the resettlement by barbarian invaders (after 500 A.D.) did an agricultural society arise that seriously challenged the domination of the land by the great forests. Two types of human communities created new uses of woodlands. The most important type was the peasant village. Living communally under the authority of a noble landowner tilling the rich lowland soils of Europe with the heavy wheeled plow they methodically pushed the forest back and produced a stable food supply for a growing population. The second type of community lived a less secure life closer to the forest. In the uplands of the British Isles and around the northern fringes of the Atlantic, remote from the trade centers of Europe, they tilled the poorer, thinner soils and relied more upon herds. They were less settled, more mobile, and for a longer time lived in and with their forests.

Early Europe was built on an abundance of forests and a technology of wood. By the time of the discovery of America, Europe had begun to encounter the problem of wood scarcity, first in the lowlands of western Europe and then in the uplands and in the great expanses of central Europe. With scarcity came a growing competition for limited resources. Peasants believed that the best use of forest lay in clearing it for crops. But the forest was also of value to the noble landowner for its products and its uses, which included a highly prized recreational value. For by the Middle Ages hunting had become an important aristocratic sport, in fact a virtual monopoly of the ruling elite.

It was this conflict of interest that set the first great restraints on the clearing and use of woodland. The noble lords, who retained legal control over all land including woodland, attempted to regulate the use of the forest. Much forest land was preserved as hunting parks, and the penalties for poaching or for tampering with such woodland were severe, including the death penalty for some offenses. Other forest land was viewed as exploitable, but it was in the interest of the lord to carefully control access to it. Licenses and payments were required from peasants to pasture pigs, to cut timber, and to till cleared land. A complicated system of forest laws arose to control the use of the forest. Peasants who made unauthorized use of it often had their houses pulled down, their crops destroyed, and themselves perhaps fined or imprisoned.

Nevertheless, there were pressures on the lords to encourge them to allow controlled clearing. If more land came under the plow and the harvest grew, a large part of that increase came to the lord in increased rents. By the 16th century so much land had been cleared that for the first time fears were expressed that Europe might experience a shortage of timber and other forest products.

This shortage was due not only to the shrinking of woodland but also to the growing demand for forest products. As Europe began to emerge from its long sleep of primitive technology, industrial activity expanded. Glassworks and soapworks needed more woodash. Mining required heavy timbers for pits and tunnels as well as charcoal for smelting. These and other industrial needs had a dramatic impact on the forest, and only with the substitution of coal as a fuel did this threat to the existence of the forest begin to recede. But coal could be effectively used only when it was "coked," and coking was not discovered until the 18th century, after much of the woodland had already been destroyed.

The discovery of the New World in the 15th century and the subsequent overseas expansion of Europe also put great pressure on the forests. Shipbuilding required enormous quantities of timber and other forest products. Oak for framing and planking, fir for masts, and "naval stores" such as pitch and tar were consumed in prodigious quantities. These demands consumed the upland forests of Britain, Ireland, and much of western Europe. With the increasing warfare of the 17th and 18th centuries, the nations of Europe turned to the woodlands of the New World as an alternative source of supply.

By the time of settlement in Colonial America, most western Europeans were unfamiliar with the wild forest. Their home was the carefully nurtured field and village. Woodland was a closely managed and regulated corner of their environment. Theirs was increasingly a world of timber scarcity. A true forest with its vast resources and its dangers was part of a distant past and an unforeseen future. For English, Scottish, and Scotch-Irish emigrants this was particularly true. They had lost their forest less than 200 years before the settlement of America began, and they had lost with it the complex forest skills and knowledge—how to work with wood, which woods are suitable for what uses, the ways of wild animals, the varieties of plants and their many uses. German settlers were more prepared to face the American forest, for in their central European homeland much of the forest still stood, and woodlore was part of their heritage. Yet, theirs was also a world of cleared fields, settled villages, landlords, and tightly-knit communities, quite different from the untamed American forests. All who came to America would be forced to change even as they altered the forest itself forever.

It was primarily the English who came first and who settled the eastern seaboard from Massachusetts to South Carolina. The great highland forests, however, blocked their advance. While these forests attracted some English and French fur traders, they seemed to fill most Europeans with misgivings, not simply because of hostile Indians, but also for the threat the forests represented to their conception of civilized life. The 18th century French settler and writer Michel de Crevecoeur expressed the feelings of many when he warned that those who settled on the forest frontier would find their lives "regulated by the wildness of the neighborhood" and would become "ferocious, gloomy, and unsocial . . . no better than carnivorous animals of a superior rank, living on the flesh of wild animals." In 1728 Colonel William Byrd of Virginia lamented that "Our country has been inhabited more than 130 years by the English, and still we hardly know anything of the Appalachian Mountains, that are nowhere above 250 miles from the sea."

Even as Byrd wrote, however, the great flow of migration that would breach the highland forest barrier had begun. The pressure of growing numbers and the hunger for land became particularly acute around the main American ports of entry—New York, Boston, Philadelphia, and Charleston. For the southern Appalachian forests, the drama of settlement began in the rich farmlands of southeastern Pennsylvania. A variety of factors drew growing numbers of immigrants to Pennsylvania: rich land, a good market for indentured labor, and close trade ties with British and European ports. By 1730 the population explosion had begun, and by 1740 most of the rich Pennsylvania piedmont had been occupied. The thousands of German and Scotch-Irish settlers who came later pushed across the Susquehanna River and by 1760 were pressed against the Blue Mountains, where the first ridges of the high Allegheny front, as well as hostile Indians, discouraged westward settlement. Pennsylvania offered many settlers a life with European roots: cleared fields, prosperous small towns, and little forest. But it was a life only a few could share as land grew scarce and prices rose. For most newcomers, the frontier beckoned. With western Pennsylvania all but closed until the Revolution, most pioneers moved southwest to Virginia, the Carolinas, and the southern highland forest.

It was in the early stages of their American experience, in Pennsylvania and in the Shenandoah Valley, that German, English, and Scotch-Irish immigrants began to learn about their new environment— new crops, new animals, new tools. There, before they met the southern Appalachian forests, they encountered the knowledge and skills of the woodsman. Most of the settlers on the American frontier in the 1700's came from environments where wood was scarce and extremely valuable. Most Scotch-Irish, for example, would have felt overwhelmed by the vastness of the American forest. They knew virtually nothing about using wood for cooking or heating and were ignorant of the skills of felling a tree, cutting it up, splitting it, or working it up into a vast array of useful tools and implements. Even the many tools associated with a wood-based material cultural, such as the axe, froe, maul, drawing knife, and adze, would have been unfamiliar. All of this changed rapidly in the open society of colonial America. Germans and Swedes taught English and Scotish-Irish, and all newcomers learned from their contacts with American Indians. Logs replaced stone in cabin construction; shingles replaced thatch, and at the family hearth, firewood replaced turf or peat. The long rifle made hunters of Europeans who had had no previous experience with guns in the Old World except possibly as soldiers.

The southern highland forest was, of course, more than a vast expanse of trees. It was a total environment—topography, soil, rivers, climate, and above all a staggering abundance of resources and unfamiliar dangers. The mountain forest had long delayed white settlement. When it finally came in a rush in the last third of the 18th century, it required new attitudes and life styles as well as skills.

One significant consequence of moving from an environment where land and forest were scarce to one where they were found in abundance was the emergence of a vision of American as the Promised Land, where not only milk and honey but also land and forest seemed limitless. In this new context the European settlers felt liberated from the constraints of their old life and especially from privileged landlords who dictated the uses of scarce resources. The new Americans saw the future stretching out unbroken before them. The image of American as the Promised Land became a powerful force, shaping the emerging society in ways that can still be felt today. And nowhere was this feeling of freedom more intense than in the great forests. Yet there was a dark side to this vision of America, for the new environment also evoked a feeling of fear and anxiety and a vision of man at war with hostile wilderness.

Ignorance of forest life and the lack of a strong woodland heritage caused European settlers to view the vast forest cover with trepidation as well as hope. The unending stretches of woodland came to represent a frightening array of dangers. Hostile Indians stimulated much of that fear in the first generation of settlement, and the variety of strange, wild animals compounded it. The mountain lion and the black bear were especially threatening in the minds of settlers in the Southern Appalachians, followed closely by the eastern timber wolf. But perhaps most horrifying of all were the snakes. Three poisonous varieties were found in the southern mountains: the eastern timber rattler, the ground rattler, and the copperhead. The Scotch-Irish in particular were frightened by these reptiles, for Ireland itself had no snakes.

In part, fear of the forest environment was the result of ignorance. Newcomers had to learn fast. Many did not, and a significant number of early settlers failed to cope. With time much of this ignorance disappeared, but many dangers were real enough. Every family had its stories, handed down for generations, of injuries, deaths, and close calls at the hands of nature. These stories suggest that the amount of stress created in the minds of the early mountain settlers from these perceived dangers must have been intense and must have created a heavy psychological burden. This stress also produced the heroic conditions which created larger-than-life figures such as Daniel Boone, John Sevier, and Simon Kenton.

Lack of a woodland tradition, combined with an abundance of land, also shaped a society unprepared to view the forest as a fragile and exhaustible resource. Instead, the settlers believed that man could do anything he wanted to the land and its wildlife, and this attitude led to an extraordinary exploitation of the woodland and its animals. Pioneer ignorance of forest management meant that they passed on a legacy of misuse with tragic consequences for the forest and for posterity. It was a true paradox, for while the early settlers were grossly wasteful of the forest, they were tightly bound to it for their very survival. They could not break through their short-term interests to see a different future.

Abundance and danger converged to shape the attitudes of the mountain forest settler along with a third factor: forest and topography imposed a powerful cultural and economic isolation. Regardless of the farming skills a family brought to their land and regardless of how rich the soil might be, the distance from the market towns and cities of the east and the difficulties of transportation imposed a new set of constraints. Well into the late 19th century mountain society was locked fast to a subsistence agriculture and an arrested social life.

In large part the new frontier culture was shaped by the attitudes which settlers brought with them, attitudes influenced by their European experience as well as their expectations of what they would find in the southern highland forest. But the mountain forest also played a decisive role. It drew the settler to it with promises of plenty but imposed sharp constraints of its own and acted to prolong a pioneer lifestyle far longer here than anywhere else.

The settlement of the Southern Appalachians began in earnest in the decade before the American Revolution. Much of this early settlement was illegal, for the British government recognized Indian rights and sought to restrain the land hungry settlers. But at the close of the Revolution, the territory west of the Blue Ridge and Allegheny Mountains quickly opened for legal settlement, and the region received a flood of new people. Some early settlers moved westward out of southern Pennsylvania, but many more traveled down the Great Wagon Road from Philadelphia to the Carolina Piedmont and through the western mountain gaps into western Virginia, Kentucky, east Tennessee, western North Carolina, South Carolina, and Georgia.

The first highland forest settlements were remarkably mobile, impermanent, and primitive. Hunting and food gathering took precedence over farming. One-third to one-half of the earliest settlers

This pioneer farmstead with its cabin, tree stumps, wandering stock, and hoe cultivation was typical of the practices suited to the land and economy of Appalachian frontier.

were transients who grew a few crops, grazed a few animals on natural vegetation, rarely bothered to legally claim the land, and moved on as the hunting grew poor. They seldom devoted much effort to improving their cabins or farmed more than a few acres. This type of settler, who never entirely disappeared from early mountain culture, was the true woodsman whose food, clothing, and shelter reflected his close alliance with the forest. He was followed quickly, however, by a permanent variety of forest farmers who formed a more stable relationship with their environment and who created the traditional southern Appalachian society.

No single ethnic group forged the pioneer life style of the southern mountains, but throughout the settlement period the Scotish-Irish from the province of Ulster in northern Ireland were at the outer edge of the advancing frontier. They were the first to move, the last to settle, and typically the most numerous people in the scattered Appalachian communities before the Civil War. Though the Scotch-Irish brought little forest tradition, they did bring an independence and an endurance to hardship that suited them well for the life they entered. Above all they brought agricultural practices and settlement patterns that, unlike those of English and German farmers, were readily adaptable to subsistence in the forest.

The agriculture of Scotland and Ireland was different from the intensive cultivation practiced in the prosperous farm villages of lowland England, and English observers invariably condemned it as primitive and inefficient. In fact, it suited the quality of lands and limited market opportunities in the north of Ireland. The system of tillage practiced in their homeland was known as infield-outfield. The infield consisted of a few of the best acres of farm, usually near the farm dwellings. Crops grown on this land were supplemented by the cultivation of the outfield. The outfield was seldom or never fertilized, was tilled for two or three years in succession and then allowed to lie fallow for several years, often returning to grass or bush, and used for pasture. Crops most frequently grown were oats, barley, and potatoes.

The diet of the Ulster family was typically supplemented with milk and butter because of a strong reliance on livestock raising. From earliest times the poor lands of Scotland and Ireland had encouraged the raising of sheep and cattle as a fundamental way of life. After crops were planted in the spring, the stock had to be tethered or more commonly would be taken to graze in rough highland pastures. Often the animals would command more of the time and attention of the farm family or community than the crops. In late October when the grain was harvested, the stock would be brought back to graze on the stubble of the infield and outfield. Ulster farming placed less emphasis upon efficiency and high yields and more upon a marginal but sustainable agriculture suited to the conditions of land, tools, and local needs.

At the same time Scotch-Irish society had remained overwhelmingly rural with little town life. The most common type of settlement was probably the clachan, or community of joint tenants, who lived in a cluster of dwellings and worked the surrounding land for a landlord. The clachan was distinctly different from the well-organized agricultural villages found in lowland England and throughout much of Europe. The former was smaller, typically a community of related families, less regulated by law and custom, more self-sufficient, and less permanent. At least until the middle of the 18th century, Ulster still had large areas of unsettled land, and settlers moved frequently. Often a family would break away from an over-settled clachan, or a clachan would grow up as a family grew. Rural life was more dispersed and individualistic than in most of Europe, but a sense of community was maintained through kinship, church gatherings, fairs, and markets. The picture we have from Ulster's past is that of a backward mixed agriculture and of mobile and independent farm settlements.

The Scotch-Irish drew heavily on this background when they encountered the highland forest with its seemingly endless supply of cheap land, few and often distant markets, and constant shortage of labor.

16

The land which the early pioneers entered was not completely covered with forests. The Indians who had lived there for centuries had cleared much of it for cultivation and hunting. Frequently, early white settlers had a choice, either to take over existing cleared areas or "old fields," or to clear their own. Though cleared land was preferred and might command higher prices, the choice was not always so obvious. Taking over cleared land implied the use of plow and manuring, a more intensive agriculture requiring a larger labor supply and aimed at selling to markets rather than family subsistence. Farming on uncleared land means girdling and burning trees, utilizing the natural fertility, and cultivating among the trees or stumps by hoe. As the soil wore out, "new ground" was cultivated and the process begun again. This slash and burn technique adopted from the Indians was well suited to a situation of plentiful land and scarce labor and was typical of the earliest frontier farming.

As for the livestock, animals were allowed to graze on any land not fenced for tillage but primarily in the woods and upland pastures. Animals were branded or otherwise marked and then turned loose to fend for themselves. The greatest attraction of this method of stock raising was that it used uncleared land to produce a commercial commodity that transported itself to distant markets. The great cattle drives to coastal cities remained a major part of the rural economy well into the 19th century.

It was not the Scotch-Irish alone who practiced this kind of frontier agriculture. It became common across the southern highlands and the frontier south. The anonymous author of *American Husbandry*, published in 1775, observed of North Carolina that "Such herds of cattle and swine are to be found in no other colonies, and when this is better settled, they will not be so common here: for at present the woods are all in common . . . In this system of crops they change the land as fast as it wears out, clearing fresh pieces of woodland, exhausting them in succession, after which they leave them to spontaneous growth . . . It presently becomes such wood as the rest of the country is: and woods here are the pasture of the cattle."

This primitive use of woodland represented a modification of a traditional Ulster agriculture and preserved the single family farm familiar to many Ulstermen. It presents a distinct contrast to the more intensive farming and highly organized villages of the English in New England and the Germans in Pennsylvania. At the same time this frontier agriculture was highly flexible and became more efficient and commercial as land grew less plentiful, labor more available, and as markets became a more important part of farming life.

As settlers, led by the Scotch-Irish, began to move into the southern

A corn crop in a deadening made in 1899.

highlands, the configuration of the mountains drew them into the river valleys, into the coves, and even to the grassy balds. But the woods were all around them, and they were faced with the problem of conquering a physical environment. The forest was only in part an enemy to be pushed aside to provide cleared fields for agriculture. It was also a tremendous resource for all manner of things. It provided them with the basic materials for establishing their rural homesteads, for making their tools and toys, for fuel, and even much of their food, for crops were always supplemented by game, wild fruits, nuts, and berries. But so much of the bounty of the forest depended on continuous woodcutting. Felling trees for building houses or for clearing land was only the beginning, for the ongoing need for wood never ceased.

All early settlers who lived as farmers were also woodsmen who had to know the forest and its secrets in order to make it yield its bounty for their agricultural practices were intimately connected with the

18

The *Fre-European Forest* was home to the Woodland tribes who, co.
1,000 BC, tapped directly into the primary nutrient cycles of the
forest.

During the *Settlement Period*, the introduction of metal tools and
domestic animals by Europeans represented a major shift in the forest
use. Settlers changed the productive capacity of the land to accomodate
grain and domestic animals.

The *Industrial Period* was marked by the introduction of technological processes capable of transforming, on a mass scale, wood as a resource into a whole range of commercial products used all over the world.

The *Contemporary Forest* is a managed resource in a society in which many contituencies have a voice in the formulation of policies which determine forest use.

Paintings by Roger Stephen

wood ands. The Scotch-Irish tradition in particular was well-suited to the forested mountains. Unlike Ulster, however, the land used for crops had first to be cleared of trees. The easiest method was slash and burn. As long as the farmer was willing to cultivate with the hoe, the remaining stumps posed little problem, for the crops, corn in particular, could be planted among them. But if the decision was made to change to cultivation with the plow and to the raising of small grains like wheat and oats, then the stumps had to be removed as well. In the situation, cutting trees, burning stumps, and grubbing out the roots required a great deal of labor.

The early settlers were also livestock raisers, and again the Ulster tradition of the Scotch-Irish played an important role in shaping the agriculture of the southern mountains. The Scotch-Irish in Ulster were accustomed to letting their animals range and especially to driving them up onto the mountain tops in the summer for grazing. The same pattern was easily transferred to the Appalachian mountains, as long as the types of animals raised were carefully chosen to fit the available range which was primarily forest. Sheep, which were common in the British Isles and throughout Europe, were rare in the early period of southern Appalachian history. Sheep were too passive to protect themselves from the predators of the forest, and they could not support themselves well on the mast (nuts and acorns) and undergrowth of the forest. Nettles and burrs entangled their wool beyond use. Only when pastures were cleared, planted in grass, and fenced could significant numbers of sheep be raised. Cattle were more adaptable to the forest and could graze on much of the undergrowth. But the preeminent southern Appalachian farm animal, the one best suited to the forest range, was the hog.

As early as the 17th century, European observers had commented on the adaptability of hogs to forest life:

> The real American hog is what is termed the wood hog; they are long in the leg, narrow in the back, short in the body, flat in the sides, with a long snout, very rough in their hair. . . . They will go to a distance from a fence, take a run, and leap through the rails three or four feet from the ground, turning themselves sidewise. These hogs suffer such hardship as no other animal could endure.

Andre Michaux, who traveled through the southern mountains in 1802, described their presence there:

> Of all domestic animals hogs are the most numerous; they are kept by all the inhabitants; several of them feed a hundred and fifty or two hundred. These animals never leave the woods, where they always find a sufficiency of food, especially

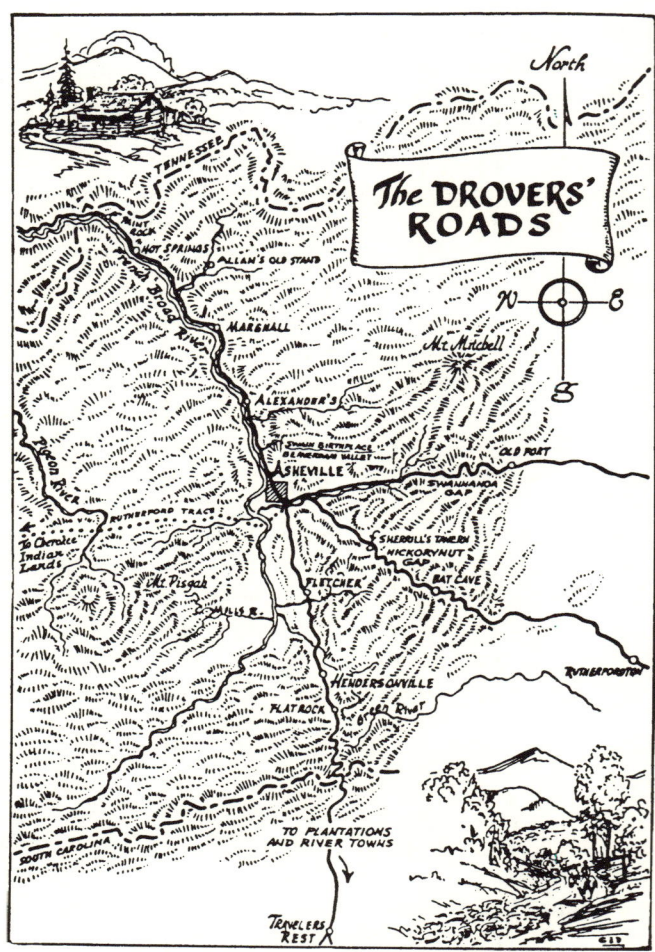

These routes were major trade arteries from the mountains into the lowlands.

in autumn and winter. They grow extremely wild, and generally go in herds. . . . Every inhabitant recognizes those that belong to him by the particular manner in which their ears are cut. They stray sometimes in the forests, and do not make their appearance again for several months; they accustom them, notwithstanding, to return every now and then to the plantation, by throwing them Indian corn once or twice a week.

Hogs thrived on the plentiful mast deposited on the floor of the highland hardwood forest, and their snouts could dredge for roots and bulbs just below the surface of the ground. In addition, hogs could defend themselves quite well against most forest predators. For these reasons, they became the dominant livestock of mountain farmers.

The forest also provided a variety of wild foods. Early frontiersmen, in the process of establishing their farms, would frequently rely on game for extended periods. Hunters perferred deer and elk to small game, for one large animal could supply the family for some time. This meat could be cut into strips and smoked and dried for "jerky," or it could be salted. Grouse and gray squirrels were considered delicacies, but a variety of other small game could be eaten as well. In order to hunt successfully, settlers not only had to be good marksmen but also had to learn the secrets of the woodland. They had to know the habits of the different species of animals and where and when they could be found. The same held true for the hunting of fruits, nuts, berries, and various edible vegetable matter.

A successful hunt provided valuable by-products such as furs, skins and fat. Furs could be used to make coats or robes, but they could also be sold to supplement the farming economy. Beaver fur was in greatest demand, but there was also a market for muskrat, gray fox, raccoon, and even possum fur. Skins, especially those of deer and elk, provided clothing and footwear. Fat had a variety of uses, not least important of which was in making greasy patches to clean and lubricate the bores of rifles. Finally, hunting offered sport as well as work. Shooting competitions and hunting as sport became a large part of the settler's relationship with the forest.

The forest provided much more than food to the pioneers. It also contained the raw material for practically everything that they needed. Houses, outbuildings, fences, tools, toys—all were made from wood. They lived in a material culture based on wood to a degree unequalled in western Europe, and unimaginable to our modern world of metal and plastic. What woods were best suited for a particular product and where to find them were part of the woodlore that had to be learned. Poplar, pine, and chestnut for log cabins, flooring, and furniture; black walnut, black cherry, and maple for the finest furniture; maple for the stocks of rifles; small crooked white oak for sled runners; what woods would bend, which was best for making pegs—all of this knowledge was vital to life in the forest. Whittling was a constant chore for settlers in this technology of wood.

Wood also had to be cut continuously for fuel. Firewood was not burned only for heat and for cooking. It was also used to heat water for washing clothes, hog killing, lard rendering, dyeing, and for making soap, maple sugar, and whiskey. Firewood was needed all year round and in prodigious quantities.

23

The forest also provided resources other than timber. Sweetners came from maple trees and from honey. Maple sap was boiled down to syrup, and "bee trees" were searched for, with swarms sometimes being captured and brought home to a homemade "bee gum" made out of a hollowed log.

Dyes also came from the forest. The two basic colors of the early settlers were blue from indigo and red from madder, both of which grew wild in the southern mountains but which also could be cultivated. Butternut, walnut, bloodroot, hickory, oak, pokeberries, sumac, oak, and goldenrod all provided various shades of yellow, brown, and green.

The forest served as a pharmacopeia to the settlers as well. A wide variety of home remedies came from the woods. Wild cherry bark was used for cough medicines, and sassafras, catnip, horehound, and pennyroyal soothed stomach troubles. Willow leaves and bark treated fever, and pine pitch healed sores and wounds. Cooked pine needles were prescribed for toothache and rhododendron oil for rheumatism.

The forest was the essential resource for sustaining a rural subsistence economy. As Thomas D. Clark has observed, "Folk use and faith in the natural products of the forest formed a seamless web of cherished belief, superstition, and quackery. Just as the woodlands contributed to man's toils and woes, they also supplied him with panaceas for his distempers, frustrations, and boredom."

Between the 1780's and the Civil War the southern highland forest had become a home to tens of thousands of families, from tenuous subsistence hunters and farmers to prosperous slave owning farmers. A network of small towns connected the region with profitable urban markets and provided a rich variety of goods that improved mountain life. Ethnic backgrounds and identities—Scotch-Irish, English, German, etc.—were largely submerged in rural mountain culture by the close of this period with the appearance of new generations and new people. Still, the first settlers had created a lifestyle based on Old Country traditions and New World environment that was inextricably tied to the woodlands. Food, clothing, building materials, medicines, and recreation were all dependent upon the forest. It was not a carefree life devoid of stress, but the abundance of the forest provided more than mere subsistence, and out of it grew eventually a more substantial society and economy.

The economy and technology of this early pioneer society were not yet sufficiently advanced to overcome the isolation of the region and pose the threat of destruction to the woodland, as was finally the case in western Europe. The growing population in the mountains did exert significant pressure on the forest, altering it, opening more and more space, and above all wasting the forest's riches. It was not until the

24

Hauling chestnut tanbark and handhewn railroad ties were two of many ways that later Appalachian settlers used the forest in the subsistence economy that was natural to the pre-industrial period.

late 19th century, when the technology of the outside world was brought fully to bear, that the highland forests were seriously threatened. Large scale timbering and mining, made economically feasible by the coming of the railroad, then raised the prospect of widespread devastation. When this more advanced technology and economy combined with the image of abundance, of the woodland as Promised Land, the result threatened the very existence of the southern Appalachian forest.

Tyler Blethen
Curtis Wood
Western Carolina University

LAND AS COMMODITY: INDUSTRIALIZATION
OF THE APPALACHIAN FORESTS, 1880-1940

A traveler through the southern mountains in the 1880's would have found a land "on the eve of a remarkable development." Still a remote but beautiful part of the southern backcountry and dominated by self-sufficient family farms, the region was on the threshold of a major era of growth in which its rich storehouse of natural resources would be developed to fuel the nation's final drive to industrial maturity. Superb timber and vast quantities of coal, iron ore, and other minerals were making the mountains the object of intense competition from both foreign and domestic capitalists intent on transforming the region into one of the "most prosperous and desirable sections" of the South. "I saw enough," wrote Charles Dudley Warner in 1888, "to comprehend why great companies, American and English, are planting themselves there and laying the foundations of cities, and why the gigantic railway corporations are straining every nerve to penetrate the mineral and forest heart of the region . . . It is a race for the prize."

In the years between the end of Reconstruction and the onset of the Second World War, Appalachia was transformed by America's race for modernization. By the millions, southern mountaineers left the family farms for "public work" in the newly constructed mining towns, logging camps, and mill villages which sprang up suddenly in the coves and hollows. The penetration of the mountains by railroads, speculators, land developers, and industrialists launched a revolution in land use and ownership that drastically altered the mountaineer's economy, society, and relationship to the land. No longer were the forests defined simply as "home" or "place"—the location of family, personal, and community values—but increasingly those within and outside of the region came to accept a more modern conception of the land as a "commodity," something to be bought and sold and used for urban-industrial purposes. Within a few short decades the forests were ravaged and exploited more intensely than in any other period of their history. As ownership and control of the land were transferred from the mountaineers to the spokesmen of the new industrial order, the fate of the region became irrevocably tied to the politics and economy of the larger society.

The transformation of mountain life had its roots in the traumatic era of the Civil War. As early as the late 1850's elements within mountain society had begun to reject the lifestyles and values orientations of their more traditional neighbors and to look outside of the mountains for more modern definitions of the good life. Located generally in the larger valleys and county seat towns, the mountain middle-class came increasingly to define progress in terms of growth and change and looked to connections with low-country merchants and politicians to provide opportunities for expanded commerce and trade. While the more traditional ridge communities remained loyal to the Union during the Civil War, the "progressive" middle-class aligned with the Confederacy and after the War played a major role in the industrial development of the region. Convinced that their own future and that of their communities lay in the exploitation of the region's mineral and timber wealth, these local entrepreneurs joined with speculators and developers from the rest of the South to promote the natural wealth of the mountains and to attract Northern and European capital.

By the turn of the century millions of acres of mountain land and forest had passed out of the hands of local residents and into the control of outside developers whose only interest was to get as much as they could out of the land and then to get out. Beginning in the late 1870's and lasting into the 1920's, the new owners of the land penetrated the mountains with thousands of miles of railroads, opening up previously isolated sections of the region and altering the traditional way of life. Land which speculators had purchased at from twenty-five cents to one dollar an acre a few years earlier, now was worth many times as much for its mineral and timber wealth. Local leaders hailed the new investments as harbingers of progress and were convinced that economic development and industrialization were best for the region's future. Most absentee developers, however, were less interested in long range economic stability than in short range profits on the land and people of the mountains.

The impact of this industrial development was profound. By 1900 the self-sufficient agricultural economy of the region had been seriously disrupted because of changing marketing, production, and land ownership patterns. Whereas the average size farm in the mountains in 1880 was about 187 acres, by 1930 the average Appalachian farm contained only 76 acres and in some countries was as low as 47 acres. Before 1880 the southern mountain family made its living directly from the land, except for modest amounts of cash which could be raised from the sale of logs, livestock, or other products. The major cash crop in the mountains was livestock, which was allowed to graze in the woodlands on

Steam powered crane loads logs near Sunburst, Haywood County, Circa 1900

Narrow gauge railroad hauls timber logs from Cherokee County, NC, circa 1910.

"common land" and driven annually to market in the low-country After 1880 the mineral and timber companies acquired much of the forested ridgeland, effectively replacing the use of the forests for agricultural and marginal logging purposes with large scale mining and timber production. The mountaineers were given jobs in the local mills, mines, and factories and easily acquired a new dependence on a cash income, canned food, and other consumer items which could be purchased at the local (often company-owned) store. For a while the boom times brought prosperity and hope for a better future, and mountain residents, like other Americans, were introduced to modern ways. But the boom was short-lived and brought not only fundamental changes in the economy and social structure of the region but also caused extensive damage to the mountain environment itself.

The Growth of Logging

One of the best examples of the effects of industrial development on the land and people of Appalachia was the great logging boom which swept the southern mountains between 1890 and 1920. As early as the 1880's outside timbermen had begun to purchase large acreages of forest land and to undertake major logging operations. In the early 1880's, for example, the Scottish Carolina Timber and Land Company with funds from capitalists in Glasgow, Scotland, and Cape Town, South Africa, built a sawmill at Newport, Tennessee, and began logging along the Pigeon River above the town. Later in the decade an Englishman, H. N. Saxton, launched the Sevierville Lumber Company in Sevier County, Tennessee, and C. F. Buffum, a Maine lumberman, opened a sawmill on the Tuskaseigee River in Jackson County, North Carolina. These companies began exporting hardwoods from the Great Smokey Mountains to Europe and pioneered the arrival of even larger firms in the years ahead.

By the 1890's the forests of the Northeast and Great Lakes regions were beginning to be depleted, and lumbermen turned increasingly to the Southern Appalachians. Large timber companies from the North purchased vast tracts of land throughout the region and began cutting the virgin ash, cherry, oak, spruce, and yellow (tulip) poplar. In North Carolina the Crosby Lumber Company of Michigan, the Foreign hardwood Log Company of New York, the Dickson-Mason Lumber Company of Illinois, and the Tuckaseigee Timber Company of New York all opened large operations in the southwestern portion of the state. Elsewhere the Asheville Lumber Company, the Parsons Pulp and Lumber Company and a host of others joined the race to tap the region's forests. After 1900 the Champion Fibre Company of Hamilton, Ohio, acquired some 300,000 acres of spruce forest, and the William Ritter Lumber Company of West Virginia operated on over 200,000 acres of timberland in western North Carolina in addition to its large holdings in other Appalachian states. In eastern Tennessee the Little River Lumber Company became a major landowner in the Smokies, and the Norwood Lumber Company, the Vestal Lumber and Manufacturing Company, and the Pennsylvania-based Babcock Lumber Company also constructed large mills. Similar companies dominated the logging operations in other Appalachian states, and by 1910 the Southern mountains produced nearly forty percent of the total timber production in the United States.

The Southern mountaineers had always utilized the surrounding forests, cutting some timber to clear fields and to construct buildings, fences, furniture, and farm implements. After the Civil War many farm families had begun to engage in the seasonal cutting of timber for sale to local sawmills. But these uses had little impact on the forests of the region since the technology was simple, and only those trees closest to the major rivers and highways could be cut. As late as 1900 as much as 75 percent of the southern Appalachian region remained in woodland,

Overland, log flume on Curtis Creek, McDowell County, NC. The flume was the least destructive method for moving timber from the upper slopes to the mill site.

and although some of the largest walnut, cherry, and other figured hardwood had been culled, most of the commercial timber was yet untouched. With the arrival of the largest companies after the turn of the century, however, new technologies and greater capital assets were brought to bear on the region's forests.

Many companies were so large that they were able to build their own railroad lines, sawmills, and logging camps deep in the timberlands. The utilization of steam-powered equipment such as Shay locomotives, overhead cableway skidders, and giant bandsaws allowed operators to cut more timber at only a fraction of the cost of earlier methods. But when used with log slides, river flumes, and splash dams, the modern techniques destroyed the streambeds and the reproductive capacities of the land. Great woods fires became almost a yearly phenomenon in the Blue Ridge, as lightning or sparks from machinery ignited sawdust and splash piles left by the loggers. The opening of many local pulp mills provided a market for the smallest trees, lending a new meaning to the term "merchantable timber," and entire mountains were clear cut and left to erode with the spring rains.

Local residents had for generations practiced the custom of "slash and burn" to clear new ground for cultivation and had annually burned

Construction of Splash Dam in Pisgah National Forest.

the forest undergrowth to provide better pasture for livestock, but the new technologies far surpassed the abilities of local farmers to exploit the land. Indeed, the total number of farms and farm acreage declined dramatically in areas of heavy outside investment as farmers sold or abandoned their farms and migrated to the camps and mill villages. Almost every timber company established one or more logging camps or sawmill towns to provide housing for labor crews in sparsely settled areas. These centers absorbed the mountain residents who sold their lands and attracted Northern and European migrants eager to benefit from the timber boom.

More than 600 company-owned towns were constructed throughout the region during these years, and in some areas they outnumbered independent, incorporated towns more than five to one. Timber towns circled the Great Smokies: Ravensford, Smokemont, Fontana, and Crestmont in North Carolina and Elkmont, Gatlinburg, Townsend, and Rittertown in Tennessee. Sunburst, North Carolina, and Tellico Plains, Tennessee, achieved populations of close to two thousand residents. Most of these towns were temporary, artificial communities in which the companies controlled almost every aspect of community life. Some offered good housing and modern conveniences, but most provided ramshackle accommodations, poor sanitation, and few amenities.

It was to these boom towns that many displaced mountaineers moved after the turn of the century, some hoping to find permanent work and avoid the hardships of sharecropping or farm tenancy, others intending to save their wages in order to return to the land as independent landowners. All would find themselves caught up in the uncertainty and dependence of the new order and would witness permanent changes in their lives, culture, and the society around them. For several years lumbering provided steady employment for thousands of mountaineers. Others found jobs in the coal mines of West Virginia, Kentucky, and Tennessee; in the mica pits and copper works of North Carolina and Tennessee; or in the textiles miles of the Carolinas and Georgia. By 1930 only about one-third of those gainfully employed in the region remained in agriculture; the rest had joined the ranks of the new industrial working class.

The prosperity that was brought by industrialization, however, was only temporary, for as rapidly as the new economic order had ascended it collapsed in the 1920's leaving the region plagued with unemployment, poverty, and destitution. The rampant overdevelopment of Appalachian resources and the frantic drive for profits with little concern for long term stability took its toll in almost all of the major industries of the region after World War I. The decline in demand for war materials and the reopening of European mines and factories (coupled with a domestic shift to oil and synthetic fibers) produced massive closings and layoffs in the American coal, mica, and textile industries. By 1919 wasteful logging practices had begun to decimate the region's forests, and in that year timber production fell to about half of its pre-war level. Increasingly in the 1920's timber companies abandoned their southern mountain properties and turned west to the unexploited timberlands of Oregon and Washington state. Those mountain families who could, returned to the land to seek out a subsistence on smaller, less productive farms; others remained in the abandoned boom towns to endure the dark years of depression. Like a train in the night, industrialization had come into the mountains raising aspirations and hopes, but when it left, it had taken most of the rich natural wealth out of the region, leaving little benefit to the mountain people themselves. What remained was a socially and economically depressed area which the rest of the nation would come to know as "Appalachia."

The human tragedy of this era was reflected in the devastation of the land itself. The once majestic ridges lay cutover and gullied; the sparkling brooks and creeks now ran full and muddy from the torrential spring rains. Major fires had burned thousands of acres of woodland and lesser fires of the undergrowth had effected at least eighty percent of the forested area. "The great mountain slopes and forest," wrote Thomas Wolfe of Asheville,

> had been ruinously detimbered; the farm-soil on the hillsides had eroded and washed down; high up, upon the hills, one saw the raw scars of old mica pits, the dump heaps of deserted mines . . . It was evident that a huge compulsive greed had been at work: the whole region had been sucked and gutted, milked dry, denuded of its rich primeval treasures; something blind and ruthless had been here, grasped, and gone. The blind scars on the hills, the denuded slopes, the empty mica pits were what was left . . . Something had come into the wilderness, and left the barren land.

The arrival of industrialization brought a new meaning and use for the Appalachian forests, one which would permanently alter the future of the mountain people. The new owners of the timberlands, lamented the Reverend Dr. A. E. Brown in 1910, "did not seem to realize they had any other value beyond what they could get for them from the lumbermen, and as the lumbermen had no other interest other than to get out of the timberlands all that was possible, no thought was given to the effect which the cutting of the timber may have on the mountain regions or looking to reforesting the area . . . Those who have destroyed the forests reaped the only benefits; those left behind, the natives, will have to bear the brunt of this work."

34

The National Forest Movement

The wanton destruction of the Appalachian forests came to national attention shortly after the turn of the century as concerned citizens such as Dr. Brown and others began to push for government intervention to conserve the remaining timberlands. Several decades earlier a nascent conservation movement had begun to lobby for the protection of the nation's forests, although most of the initial interest was in the protection of public lands in the West. Large timber companies that had acquired thousands of acres of the public domain (often by subterfuge and fraud) had begun to turn much of that land into wasteland. In 1876 Congress established the Division of Forestry in the Department of Agriculture, and in 1891 it passed the National Forest Reserve Act granting the president the power to set aside portions of the public domain as "forest reserves." By 1900 some 35 million acres of western timberland had been designated for protection. Since federal legislation provided no funds for the acquisition of private property, and since little public land remained in the more heavily populated East, all of the new National Forest reserves lay in the public domain west of the Mississippi.

In 1900, however, the Division of Forestry in cooperation with the Geological Survey of the U. S. Department of the Interior conducted a field investigation of the southern Appalachian region. The survey results were sent to Congress in 1902 by President Theodore Roosevelt who described the widespread damage that had occurred in the region's forests. In the logging operations of the southern mountains, the survey reported,

> There has naturally been no thought for the future. Trees have been cut so as to fall along the line of least resistance regardless of what they crush. Their tops and branches, instead of being piled in such a way and burned at such a time as would do the least harm, are left scattered among the adjacent growth to burn when driest, and thus to destroy or injure everything within reach. The home and permanent interests of the lumberman are generally in another state or region, and his interests in these mountains begins and ends with the hope of profit.

In order to stop the continuing loss of these resources, the survey recommended the creation of a Federal Forest Reserve in the Southern Appalachians and the introduction of scientific forest management practices.

Ironically, it was in these same forests that the idea of practical forestry was inaugurated in the United States. In 1889 George

Washington Vanderbilt, the wealthy grandson of Commodore Cornelius Vanderbilt of New York, visited Asheville for his health and was so impressed with the area that he began to acquire land southwest of the town on which to build a summer estate. Vanderbilt hired the renowned New York architect Richard Morris Hunt and the premier landscape architect Frederick Law Olmsted to design and construct a French Renaissance-style castle unequaled anywhere in America. Biltmore House, as he called his 250 room castle, was filled with rare paintings, tapestries, porcelain, and antiques from Europe and surrounded by elegant gardens, greenhouses, and a conservatory. At Olmsted's suggestion, a "model village" was built near the entrance to the estate, housing a hospital, stores, and a church.

Vanderbilt also employed a young Pennsylvania forester named Gifford Pinchot, the future chief of the U. S. Forest Service, to supervise Biltmore's forest lands. Determined to show a profit from the careful management of his forests, Vanderbilt purchased a "private game reserve" of 100,000 acres of virgin timber adjacent to the castle, renaming it the Pisgah Forest. Under Pinchot's direction, reforestation of cutover and eroded areas on the estate was begun, and selective logging was undertaken at the foot of Mt. Pisgah.

Pinchot left Biltmore in 1895 and was succeeded by Carl Alwin Schenck, a young, highly recommended German forester, who for fourteen years carried on and intensified Pinchot's efforts. Schenck continued the practice of selective lumbering, introduced new logging techniques, and expanded reforestation efforts throughout the Vanderbilt estate. In 1898 Schenck carried out one of Pinchot's recommendations by establishing the Biltmore School of Forestry in which he personally trained young men in all aspects of practical and textbook forestry. Schenck, like Pinchot, emphasized not just preservation but forest management practices that would assure the continued production of saleable timber. During Schenck's years at Biltmore, the Vanderbilt properties were among the leading producers of hardwood timber in the region. Unfortunately, Vanderbilt's practical forestry model was not accepted by other logging operations. Schenck was able to convince nearby Champion Fibre Company to introduce sustained-yield forestry on its Pigeon River properties, but most companies were less interested in forest management than in maximizing production.

Therefore, by the time the survey of the southern Appalachian forests was submitted to Congress in 1902, an influential group of conservation-minded Americans had begun to favor the creation of eastern forest reserves. Led by Gifford Pinchot himself, who had become Chief of the USDA Division of Forestry in 1898, conservationists submitted nearly fifty bills to Congress between 1900 and 1910 to authorize

Dr. and Mrs. Schenck in Pisgah Forest.

the creation of an Appalachian Forest Reserve. Throughout the decade the movement grew in size and diversity to include a variety of organizations including the Appalachian National Park Association, formed in Asheville by Dr. Chase P. Ambler, the national Sierra Club, the National Hardwood Lumber Association, and the powerful American Forestry Association. Despite this broad-based support, however, Congress continued to reject such legislation on the basis of opposition ranging from State's rights to the constitutional question of the Federal government's authority to acquire land for national forests.

Nor were the conservationists themselves united on the legislation. Indeed, the conservation movement embodied at least two distinct groups, the preservationists and the utilitarians, each of which held a different conception of the meaning and use of the nation's forests. One, inspired by Henry Thoreau and exemplified by John Muir, the founder of the Sierra Club, believed in saving as much as possible of the nation's scenic forests just as they were—never to be exploited by man. These preservationists hoped that large sections of southern Appalachian timberland could be protected from all commercial activities, including logging and mining, and set aside for recreational and scenic purposes. In addition to preserving the natural heritage of the country, they argued, the national forests ought to provide an "escape" from the "industrial pace" of urban life.

The other conservationists faction, the utilitarians, favored the continued use of the forests for economic purposes, albeit under the protection and careful management of the Federal government. The majority of the leaders of the conservation movement, including its most renowned leaders, Gifford Pinchot and Theodore Roosevelt, perceived the primary purpose of the forest reserves to be the protection and management of timber resources for commercial production. "Forest reserves," wrote Pinchot in 1905, "are for the purpose of preserving a perpetual supply of timber for home industries, preventing destruction of the forest cover which regulates the flow of streams, and protecting local residents from unfair competition in the use of forest and range." It was this latter group, led by Pinchot and the Department of Agriculture, that would eventually succeed in achieving the passage of the Weeks Act in 1911 authorizing the Secretary of Agriculture to purchase private lands in the East for national forest reserves. The preservationists would see their dream fulfilled in the late 1920's and 1930's when the Federal government, through the Department of the Interior, acquired land in the southern mountains for the Great Smokey Mountains National Park and the Blue Ridge Parkway.

Conflict within the conservation movement, between advocates of "scenic preservation" and supporters of "economic forestry," continued to complicate the management of the national forests and subsequently had a major impact upon land use practices in the southern Appalachian region. But common threads which bound the two groups together played an even more important role in shaping the future of the mountains and reflected the emergence of a more modern value-orientation toward the land. Both factions approached the issue of conservation from a decidedly nationalistic and predominantly urban perspective. National needs, whether they were those of the tourist, the scientist, or the industrialist, were given priority over local concerns. The popular image of the mountaineer as backward, degenerate, and uncivilized seemed to justify this attitude, placing power in the hands of those who seemed "best equipped" to bring progress to the region. For many urban progressives, the creation of national forests in Appalachia became the easiest way to protect the resources they most coveted and the best way to bring the mountaineers into the modern age.

The passage of the Weeks Act and the subsequent purchase of timberland by the Federal government initially stirred little popular reaction in the mountains. A few business leaders voiced optimism that the forest reserves would boost tourism and insure a perpetual supply of timber, but most local residents reacted indifferently to the legislation. Most of the land being studied for acquisition had already passed out of the hands of local people and into the control of timber companies and other corporations. The initial acquisition of land, moreover, was limited by law to large tracts of "high quality" ridgeland located on the headwaters of navigable streams. Such tracts generally did not include farmland or residences and were usually purchased from lumber companies or land investors. In fact one of the first tracts purchased was 87,000 acres of Vanderbilt's Pisgah Forest, which when combined with other property in 1916 became the first eastern national forest, the Pisgah National Forest. In 1918 the Pisgah was joined by three

The Entrance to Pisgah National Forest.

39

more such forests—the Shenandoah and the Natural Bridge in Virginia, and the White Mountain in New Hampshire. Two years later five more forests were created in Appalachia—the Boone (now part of the Pisgah); the Nantahala in North Carolina, South Carolina, and Georgia; the Cherokee in Tennessee; the Unaka in North Carolina, Tennessee, and Virginia; and the Monongahela in West Virginia.

By 1920 the Forest Service had acquired over two million acres of Appalachian forestland, including over 250,000 acres in western North Carolina alone. Most of the land was purchased at from $5 to $10 per acre; over seventy percent of the land eventually acquired was severely cutover or burned. The logging companies, having purchased the land from local residents for as little as 25¢ to $2 per acre and having removed millions of board feet of marketable timber, were usually eager to unload what scholars have called "the lands nobody wanted." It now became the responsibility of the government to rehabilitate these forests for new and different purposes.

During the 1920's and into the 1930's the Federal government followed a two pronged policy in its relationship to the southern Appalachian forests. On the one hand, the Forest Service and later such New Deal agencies as the Civilian Conservation Corps launched a massive program of reforestation which in turn spurred a remarkable regeneration of second growth forest in the region. This effective government planning not only provided potential long-term economic benefits but protected the forest environment and contributed to the survival of elements of the traditional Appalachian culture. On the other hand, continued expansion of national forest lands and the purchase of additional lands by the Tennessee Valley Authority and the National Park Service brought increasing conflict with local mountain people. As greater quantities of land were purchased and as larger numbers of small farms and ancestral homesteads were acquired, local hostility to these government agencies continued to grow and would be manifest in a variety of ways for decades to come.

One area of the Forest Service's responsibility, for example, was the regulation of grazing, fire protection, and rehabilitation of the mountain forests. Rangers not only had to locate and survey purchased property, but they had to convince local farmers to end the age old practice of annually burning the woodlands to improve pasture for their livestock. Many residents believed that if they were stopped from burning-out the woods, they would cease to have adequate range and the insects and other pests would destroy the crops. Others were angered at the newly imposed fees placed on livestock grazing in public lands. The Forest Service, of course, was less sympathetic with these local customs and was determined to control fires and implement forest

40

management practices. Consequently, animosity continued to grow and was reflected in the rising number of intentionally set woods fires which plagued the region.

After 1924, moreover, the rapid growth of Federal landownership in the mountains helped to fuel the growing disillusionment and anger of local residents. Indeed the greatest growth in the total number of land purchases in Appalachia came in the 1920's and 1930's as the Forest Service sought to consolidate its holdings and acquired hundreds of small parcels throughout the region. By 1940 the Forest Service controlled over five million acres of land in Appalachia. Many farm families were happy to sell marginal land upon which it had become difficult to survive, but others resented the government's interference with their lives.

The creation of the Great Smokey Mountains National Park and the Blue Ridge Parkway, and the construction of TVA dams in the 1930's resulted in the condemnation of hundreds of mountain farms and in the relocation of thousands of mountain families. The Tennessee Valley Authority, for example, displaced more than 3,000 families in the construction of Norris Dam in East Tennessee and more than 1,300 families in the building of Fontana Dam in western North Carolina. Coming as they did in the midst of the Depression, these actions convinced some mountain residents that the Federal government was following a well-laid plan to destroy the mountain way of life. In the minds of many local people, the purchase of mountain land for national forests, lakes, and parks had not only contributed to the depression of the local agricultural and timber economy, but it was also depriving a hard-hit people of their last chance at independent survival. The government's acquisition of large numbers of small farms sold at sheriff's auctions for nonpayment of taxes seemed to support these feelings of suspicion, hostility, and despair.

The frustration that gripped many mountaineers in the late 1930's as they faced an uncertain future was evident in the correspondence of William Wirt, a mountain farmer from Epperson, Tennessee. In 1938 Wirt wrote a letter to a New York friend in which he described the dramatic changes that had occurred in the mountains. Living in a remote cove at the foot of the Great Smokies, he had witnessed the arrival of the railroads, the logging boom, and now the coming of the TVA. The construction of Fowler Dam near Murphy, North Carolina, he noted, was providing temporary work for many of the local men, but the dam would inundate some of the finest farmland in the county. "What would become of the people," he wondered, and where would the extra revenues come from to pay for county government and for the education of the children? He lamented the arrival of the new age:

One day we were the happiest people on the earth. But like the Indian we are slowly but surely being driven from the homes that we have learned to love, and down to the man we are not a friend of the Government for the simple reason that every move they have made has increased our poverty.

We were told that if we kept the fire out of the forest that we would have plenty of range for our cattle, but we found that after a few years that there is no range left. We were also told that we would have plenty and increasing flow of water in our mountain streams furnishing an abundance of fish for sport and food. But I've found that our streams are drying up and the fish in the ponds that are left are all dying, and at times you can smell them as you pass along the highway. Fifteen years ago you could have seen in the forest here thousands of cattle, sheep and hogs. Today you never see one out in the forest, and if you do his head and horns is the heaviest part about him.

Now what are we going to do, move on and try to fit in where we do not belong or undertake to face the situation and gradually starve to death? In the little mountain churches where we once sat and listened to the preaching of the gospel with nothing to disturb us, we now hear the roar of machinery on the Sabbath day. After all I have come to believe that the real old mountaineer is a thing of the past and what will finally take our place, God only knows.

For the people and the forests of the Southern Appalachians the coming of industrialization had brought permanent and enduring change. A more modern meaning of the land and forests as commodity, the technological ability to exploit vast quantities of natural resources, and the insatiate appetite of human greed had combined to reek devastation on the land and economic depression on the people of the region. The enlargement of the Federal government's role in protecting and managing the forests brought some order to the chaos, but it also introduced new interest groups and new uses for the region's resources. For the mountain population, the industrialization of the Appalachian forests had not only altered the cultural meaning of the forests, but it had shifted the political power over the use of the woodlands from a regional to a national base. This shift in political power, a by-product of modernization throughout America, would result in continuing conflict between local needs and national desires in the decades to come.

Ronald D. Eller
Mars Hill College

SOUTHERN APPALACHIAN FORESTS: THE LAST FIFTY YEARS

Some two thousand years ago Pliny, a grand old Roman philosopher, made a remark which is just as pertinent for us today as it was then: "The trees have a thousand uses, all of which are indispensable to the full enjoyment of life." And yet, for all of that indispensability, modern Americans have a difficult time realizing the absolute importance of trees to their lives. Sadly, all too many of us, to quote the ancient proverb, "can't see the forest for the trees." Yet it is our good fortune to be blessed, as few others are blessed, with an incomparable variety and abundance of great forests. It is impossible to walk, ride, or fly anywhere in the southeastern United States without encountering the remnants of a great forest. And in Southern Appalachia the forest is so prominent that it is and has been a major determinant in the shaping of millions of lives.

Since the dawn of human history, man has been vitally influenced by the forest. Indeed, from the earliest accounts of history, we are told that man, keenly aware of the importance of trees to his survival, actually worshipped them. The Bible speaks of the Tree of Knowledge. The oak was sacred to the Romans, as laurel was to the Greeks. And out of the forests of Germany came the idea for our modern day Christmas tree. Our use of holly to celebrate Christmas has ancient roots, going back to the Romans who used it to mark their doors as a sign of festivity. And what bride hasn't wished for the smell of orange blossoms, the international symbol of wedding bliss? Even our hopes for peace are reflected in a forest symbol: the logo of the United Nations is a globe encircled by two sprigs of olive, the symbol of peace. The forest has also grown into our tongue: "Spare the rod and spoil the child"; "As the twig is bent, so inclines the tree." But our own beloved Whittier, with his Quaker touch, said it most meaningfully in his "The Barefoot Boy": "I was rich in flowers and trees, humming birds and honey bees."

We have indeed been rich in flowers and trees. Yet it behooves us to take to heart a reminder given by Stewart Udall when he was Secretary of the Interior: "Each generation has its own rendezvous with the land." The legacy we inherited from the previous generations was, at best, a mixed blessing. Certainly the forests which were passed on to us in the 1930's would have had a hard time qualifying as precious heirlooms. Indeed, those 1930's woodlands were in such pathetic shape that they merited the name "the lands nobody wanted." Yet it has been the destiny of this generation to have its rendezvous with that land and that forest. And, wonderfully enough, that rendezvous has produced a citizenry that is absolutely unparalelled in history for its concern about the forests and lands it inherited.

Prior to the 1930's the average citizen regarded the forest as a bountiful natural resource treasury from which to extract anything he needed in the way of material wants—food, shelter, clothing, paper, fuel, furniture, and anything else his inventive mind could convert the forest into for personal gain or comfort. But today the function and role of the forest is viewed with a much wider and much more encompassing eye—an eye that sees campgrounds, fishing streams, hiking trails, and a whole new world of recreational applications as well as watersheds and timberlands. The changes are perhaps best illustrated by contrasting the views of two users of the Appalachian forest. The timber baron of the 1890's saw the forest as a plum for the picking, shouted "TIMBER!," and picked it clean. On the other hand, a stately old hiking man, United States Supreme Court Justice William O. Douglas, avidly sought out the forest as an adventure and as an escape from the frustrations of daily city living. "A people who climb the ridges and sleep under the stars in high mountain meadows, who enter the forest and scale the peaks, who explore the mountains—these people will give their country some of the indomitable spirit of the mountains," he wrote.

But it took a monstrous world depression, a horrible world war, and a series of environmental catastrophes to bring about this change in attitude. The great world depression of 1929 came on the heels of unprecedented environmental disasters throughout the United States. An unrelenting erosion of the soil was draining the very life-giving nutrients from millions of acres of land. The Great American West had become the Great American Dust Bowl. And lands which once were occupied by magnificent forests had become awesome wastelands— gutted, burned over eye-sores. As one conservationist put it, "In a sense, the great depression was a bill collector sent by nature, and the darkest tidings were borne on every silt-laden stream and every dust cloud that darkened the horizon."

One of the regions most disasterously stricken by both the great depression and the multiple environmental catastrophes was the Appalachian South and its people. When Franklin Delano Roosevelt, characterizing the evils which beset the nation, spoke of "one third of a nation ill-housed, ill-clad, ill-nourished" he could not have more precisely described conditions in the Appalachian forest lands.

However, it was to be the good fortune of both Appalachia and the nation itself to witness the coming into the White House in 1933 of a President who prided himself on being both a politician and a strong conservationist. Indeed, Franklin Delano Roosevelt once listed himself in *Who's Who* as a "tree grower." He had spent a lifetime improving the soil and forests on his personal estate, Hyde Park. As governor of New York, he had initiated a new forestry program for the whole state. He loved the forest and woodlands and once described them as "the lungs of our land, purifying our air and giving fresh strength to our people."

As president of the United States, he quickly demonstrated that he was well aware of conservation needs—both of man and land. With his administration came the launching of the second major nationwide conservation movement. His cousin, Theodore, had launched a similar movement for the preceding generation. Two of the most important conservation measures ever undertaken in this nation were begun under Franklin Roosevelt—the Civilian Conservation Corps and the Tennessee Valley Authority. Both were deeply concerned with the rehabilitation of the devastated forest and soil resources of the nation.

President Roosevelt was well aware of the Weeks Act of 1911 which had been so instrumental in establishing the national forests in the Eastern United States. He was also well aware that those eastern national forests needed an enormous amount of work if they were to become true, highly productive forests. In a press conference at the White House March 15, 1933, shortly after taking office, Roosevelt told news reporters that, "Taking it all through the East where, of course, the unemployment is relatively the worst with far more people, nearly all of the so-called forest land owned by the Government is second, third, or fourth growth land—what we call scrub growth . . . little bits of trees, saplings, and so forth. Proper forestation is not possible." But he quickly reassured them that with proper management and with sufficient timber stand improvement, "those trees then eventually will become a very valuable lumber corp."

And he had the answer to the situation—an answer that would take care of the scrub forests and of unemployment. That answer was to establish a civilian conservation corps utilizing the millions of unemployed young Americans and putting them to work in those scrub forests. In the process two things would be rehabilitated, he said: the young men and the land. He became almost infatuated with the idea and conveyed it to almost anybody who would listen. One of his most important listeners was the United States Congress, which, concerned about mass unemployment and the plight of millions, broke all records in enacting the necessary legislation to implement the President's civilian conservation idea. On March 21, 1933 the bill was introduced in Congress, and it became law on March 31, 1933, officially creating what has ever since been known as the Civilian Conservation Corps.

As the proposal was making its way through Congress, numerous criticisms arose, including a charge that the bill was anti-labor and, if passed, would provide cheap government-sponsored labor in competition with open market private labor, thereby reducing wages for forest workers. On the other hand, its champions successfully rebutted that it was a *relief* rather than an *employment* bill, that it was a conservation measure which would create profitable forests, provide fire protection for existing forests, prevent floods and erosion, and protect the new second growth forests in the South.

In the weeks preceding the introduction of the bill, Roosevelt had done an enormous amount of investigative work, plumbing the actual and potential needs for a conservation crops. Every national forest supervisor and every national park superintendent was directed to do an indepth inventory and spell out in labor terms or man-power hours what it would take to rehabilitate his forest or park and put it into first class condition. As an incentive, the officials were alerted to the prospect that, if funds became available, their particular unit would receive all the labor necessary to do all the things they had always dreamed of doing. These inventories were fed into the President's staff in Washington and became most instrumental in getting the conservation bill enacted.

In the meantime, in accordance with the President's desires, the Civilian Conservation Crops was immediately activated. He assigned the United States Department of Labor the responsibility for recruiting the young men, and this was quickly done by calling upon each state's welfare agency to select and provide its assigned quota of enrollees, as the conservation corpsmen came to be called. Following the recruitment, the United States Army was assigned the task of taking the enrollees and conditioning them. This included providing them with uniforms, discipline, food, and the necessary vaccinations to make them healthy. This usually took about two weeks. At the end of this period of time, the young men were turned over to what became known as the "Using Service," which, in those early days, meant either the National Park Service or the United States Forest Service. It is worthy of note that the reason Roosevelt designated the use of the foregoing agencies was that he felt that they were the only ones who could handle the emergency mobilization of his "tree army."

46

In accordance with the President's plans, the first enrollee was selected on April 7, 1933, and the first camp was erected on April 17, 1933, very appropriately in the George Washington National forest, a short distance from Washington, D. C.—easy visiting distance for the President. Within three months some 300,000 persons were at work in 1,468 Civilian Conservation Corps camps scattered across the nation. The forests of Southern Appalachia, for the first time in their history, received a mass of laborers whose sole interest was in healing rather than in destroying.

The implementation of the Civilian Conservation Corps struck at the most vital heart strings of humanity. President Roosevelt, in his message to Congress requesting the establishment of the Corps, had emphasized that "It will conserve our precious natural resources. It will pay dividends to the present and future generations. It will make improvements in national and state domains which have been largely forgotten in the past few years of industrial development. More important, however, than the material gains will be the moral and spiritual value of such work."

From the coves and valleys of the Appalachian mountains, as well as from the towns and villages, thousands of unemployed youngsters made their way to a Civilian Conservation Corps camp in the years 1933-1942. For example, at least sixty of North Carolina's one hundred counties had a camp, and over seventy thousand of her sons served in those camps or others like them across the nation. Each camp enrolled about two hundred men and was organized like a military unit, with tents or barracks for living quarters, a mess hall (kitchen-dining room), infirmary, recreation hall, and numerous utility buildings. While in camp, the young men were under the supervision of military officers, including a commanding officer and a camp physician. For work assignments they were turned over each morning to a civilian superintendent and his assistants.

By mid-April, 1933, local newspapers everywhere began publishing articles about the "CCC," as the Civilian Conservation Corps was quickly called. The CCC became big news because it was bringing new jobs and new money into hundreds of communities. The Bryson City Times, for example, ran banner headlines, "318 Men Arrive in Bryson City." States having national forests or national parks, such as North Carolina and Tennessee in Southern Appalachia, were the recipients of a very large number of camps and enrollees. The newly established Great Smoky Mountains National Park and the Weeks Law national forests, such as Pisgah and Nantahala and Cherokee, had improvement needs which were perfectly suited to the great employment needs of the Civilian Conservation Corps. As a result, many of the counties in western North Carolina had as many as two, three, and even four camps at one time. Never before in the history of forestry had there been so many laboring hands to invest in one assignment—improve the forests!

To the forests of Southern Appalachia came an army of young laborers. They came from all walks of life and with a remarkable variation of education and skills. All of them were from backgrounds of despair and were seeking a singularly new life. For many of them, it was the first time they had ever been away from home. Everything, from the food to social life, to new companions and new work assignments contained a new challenge, adventure, and opportunity. For the first time in their lives, many of the boys were exposed to such social amenities as deodorant, tooth-paste, daily baths, and balanced diet. Furthermore, the Civilian Conservation Corps offered each member an opportunity for learning a vocation such as heavy equipment operator, powder-man, radio operator, chef, auto mechanic, or whatever appealed to him. In addition, thousands of enrollees learned to read and write while they were in camp. That was not all; every enrollee, exposed to regular hours and a superb offering at the dining table, gained weight and improved in health. Also, recreation was a bonus for most of the men. An on-going recreational program offered athletic sports, especially boxing, basketball, and baseball. Inter-camp rivalry in all these sports became extremely competitive and became an additional means of instilling pride and esprit de corps.

But it was the world of forest work that filled their lives five days of the week. And that work was remarkably diverse. For example, in the Pisgah National Forest, work assignments ranged from deer-keeper to trout-keeper. Pisgah National Forest happened to be one of the few forests that still retained a stock of deer. Thanks to the far-sighted efforts of George W. Vanderbilt, the original owner of Pisgah Forest, wild-life, such as deer, had been protected and sheltered during a period when it had been all but exterminated in other southern forests. Realizing the significance of this, the Forest Service decided to use Pisgah National Forest as a breeding ground for re-stocking deer throughout the forests of the South. So the CCC boys became nurse-maids to a forest full of deer. They joined together as census-takers and ran a tally on how many deer were in their forest. Then they rounded up a number of fawns, established feeding pens for them, and, using a standard baby formula, nursed those fawns around the clock, just as a mother would have nursed a new born baby. They, as might have been expected, made pets out of the fawns, gave them fancy names such as "Shirley Temple," and became as attached to them as if they were members of their own family. But eventually, when the fawns had attained sufficient maturity to forage for themselves, they were loaded up and shipped off to other forests. One of the CCC boys recently recalled those days: "We were taking a load of those deer down to Florida and got pulled over by a suspicious highway trooper in Georgia. He thought we were carrying a load of mountain moonshine. And he knew we were flat out lying when he asked us what we were hauling and we said, 'deer.' You should have seen the look on his face when he lifted up the truck cover and saw the bunch of deer!"

Every deer successfully transplanted from the Pisgah National Forest meant an improvement in the wildlife offering of a new southern forest. And today throughout the South, many a hunter, hiker, and family out sightseeing get the fabulous thrill of seeing a deer in its natural habitat, thanks to the work of those CCC boys and the vision of Franklin D. Roosevelt.

As to the "trout-keepers," previous census statistics had indicated that the Appalachian forest streams were greatly understocked and were in dire need of replenishing with new brood stock of trout and other game fish. Thus, as part of its conservation program, the Forest Service, in cooperation with the State Wildlife division, using CCC funds and labor, established trout farms and as diligently nourished them as it had the deer. Stream after stream throughout the forests of Appalachia was stocked and restocked with game fish. Today, thanks to the efforts of the CCC boys and their supervisors, the trout streams of our eastern forests are the favorite fishing spots for thousands. Indeed, the most recent data show that for 1983 alone, in the national forests of North Carolina, almost 300,000 fishermen wet their lines, enjoying a sport that was tremendously enriched by the labors of boys long since departed.

But the deer and the fish are only a tiny part of the forest story so far as the Civilian Conservation Corps is concerned. A recent author made the statement that "The national forests of the East, in the main, were assembled from land that nobody wanted. Nearly all were land that had been abused, poorly protected, or ignored, whose owners were happy to unload them on the Federal government." But today, little more than half century later, those same lands are described as "a treasure store of scenic, timber, wildlife, mineral, wilderness, and recreational resources." Not surprisingly it has also been said that the able management of the United States Forest Service in successfully rehabilitating those forests was one of the greatest achievements in the history of conservation. But what has not been said, what is not generally publicized, nor generally appreciated is that it was the work, the rejuvenation work, of the Civilian Conservation Corps boys that converted those scrub forests into a "treasure store."

In forests everywhere the healing hand of the CCC program was

Black Logger in Pisgah Forest, 1940.

felt. The current beauty of the Cherokee, the Nantahala, the Pisgah, or the George Washington National Forest, or any of them for that matter, is directly attributable to the millions of hours of work expended on them by the CCC enrollees from 1933 to 1942. Neither Gifford Pinchot nor Carl Alwin Schenck, who pioneered professional forestry in Southern Appalachia, could have envisioned the thousands of laborers which the Civilian Conservation Corps assigned to the very region where they had labored and planned the nation's first scientific forestry program. Terms that those two men had learned in European forestry schools found application at the hands of young American men who had never had a day's schooling in forestry. But the timber stand improvement brought about by their labors was as effective as either of the old foresters could have expected or demanded. While teaching at the Biltmore Forest School on the Vanderbilt Estate, Schenck had repeatedly told his forestry students, "Remove that ugly, misshapen tree and give that young one the chance to grow!" "Plant carefully!" "Save the land!" This was exactly what the CCC boys did, not only in the forests of the Appalachian ranges but throughout this entire nation.

On every major forest under the careful guidance of a trained forester, the CCC enrollees diligently constructed hiking trails, cut out weed trees, removed misshapen scrubs, built fire towers, constructed fire roads, improved streams, fought fires, built picnic areas, erected bridges, and accomplished a host of other tasks necessary to allow nature to flourish and produce a bountiful and highly useful forest—a forest useful for both economic and recreational purposes. The end result was the forests that are providing today's generation with a cornucopia of benefits, all directly or indirectly related to the rejuvenation labors of the CCC project.

Just as thousands of CCC-ers labored in the nation's forests so did similar thousands apply their healing skills to the national parks. For example, the Great Smoky Mountains National Park was very new in 1933 and was in dire need of much labor to rehabilitate the woodlands which had only recently been widely timbered by the big lumber companies. Throughout the entire park, millions of man-hours of labor were needed to make it possible for the park to fulfill the mission for which it had been set aside—a national pleasuring ground featuring a beautiful forest and a bountiful wildlife.

From all over the South and from the streets of New Jersey and New York, came Civilian Conservation Corps enrollees to labor on beautifying the park. A 1937 enrollee in Camp NP-4, Company 3453, Smokemont, detailed some of the work he and his companions were doing: "A large camping area and future trailer camp to accommodate hundreds of tourists is under construction. A nursery is maintained. Trails both foot and horseback, roadside beautification, telephone line maintenance, bridges, and other phases of forestry and conservation are outstanding accomplishments." Multiply that work by nine years and thousands of man-hours, and it is easy to appreciate the fact that much of the current beauty of the Great Smokies is a result of the labor of those young men almost half a century ago. And for those who enjoy the beauty of the Blue Ridge Parkway and the delightful sense it gives of being in and out of the forest, it is well to remember that they, too, are the beneficiaries of the laborers of the CCC who diligently landscaped the Parkway and planted so skillfully that it all looks natural today.

In the meantime the Tennessee Valley Authority was also very busy utilizing Civilian Conservation Crops labor to check erosion and to plant millions of young trees, thereby improving the watershed for the Tennessee Valley. Its enrollees spent their working hours trying to remedy the hideous erosion scars which very poor farming and timbering techniques had brought upon the land. Trees were planted on every acre that could be made available by local owners. And all the art of conservation science was applied throughout the area to insure that the erosion was checked and the land's fertility renewed. When the TVA's CCC program was closed out in 1942, it had planted millions of trees. Indeed, between the CCC and the local farmers who were encouraged by the TVA authorities to convert their old fields into new forests, two hundred million trees were planted in the region. These, of course, are trees which have given the region its beauty, but they also soaked up the rain and thereby helped to prevent floods.

Man's rendezvous with the land continued and brought him face to face with another war—the all encompassing World War II. Part of that rendezvous included the CCC boys who had labored in the forests. Their training and discipline had ideally prepared them for the military service—another bonus from what had been designed as purely a conservation program. Those boys wound up in all branches of military service and served all over the world. As they went off to war, some of their conservation work in the forests was taken up by conscientious objectors, many of whom moved into camps recently vacated by the CCC boys. The never ending task of fire-fighting was taken over, partially at least, by the conscientious objectors, as was trailbuilding and all the other activities forest use and protection demanded. For example, throughout the southern Appalachian forests, the chestnut blight had devastated what had once been magnificent stands of chestnut groves. The CO's, as they were commonly called, were assigned the task of removing those dead chestnuts lest they become fire hazards. All along the Blue Ridge Parkway, the Smokies, etc., they labored, removing thousands of skeleton trees and making an opening for nature's replacements in the forests.

The coming of World War II made very evident the remarkable value of our forests. Indeed, according to Lyle F. Watts, America's chief forester at that time, "World War II proved that wood is just as essential to victory as steel, aluminum, or coal." Then, because the military swallowed up every available ton of metal, enormous demands were placed upon the nation's forests. So great were those demands that the period has been called "a lumber man's carnival" because there was a market for practically everything the forest produced. The forests of Southern Appalachia made a unique contribution to the war effort: dead chestnut trees were harvested by the thousands and used as a source of tannic acid, the acid essential for tanning the leather which went into millions of pairs of boots for the American soldiers.

When those victorious soldiers returned from overseas, they came with new wants, new demands, and new values. Thus, shortly after World War II, there came new demands upon the forest and all of our natural resources. Out of those demands came environmental awareness

52

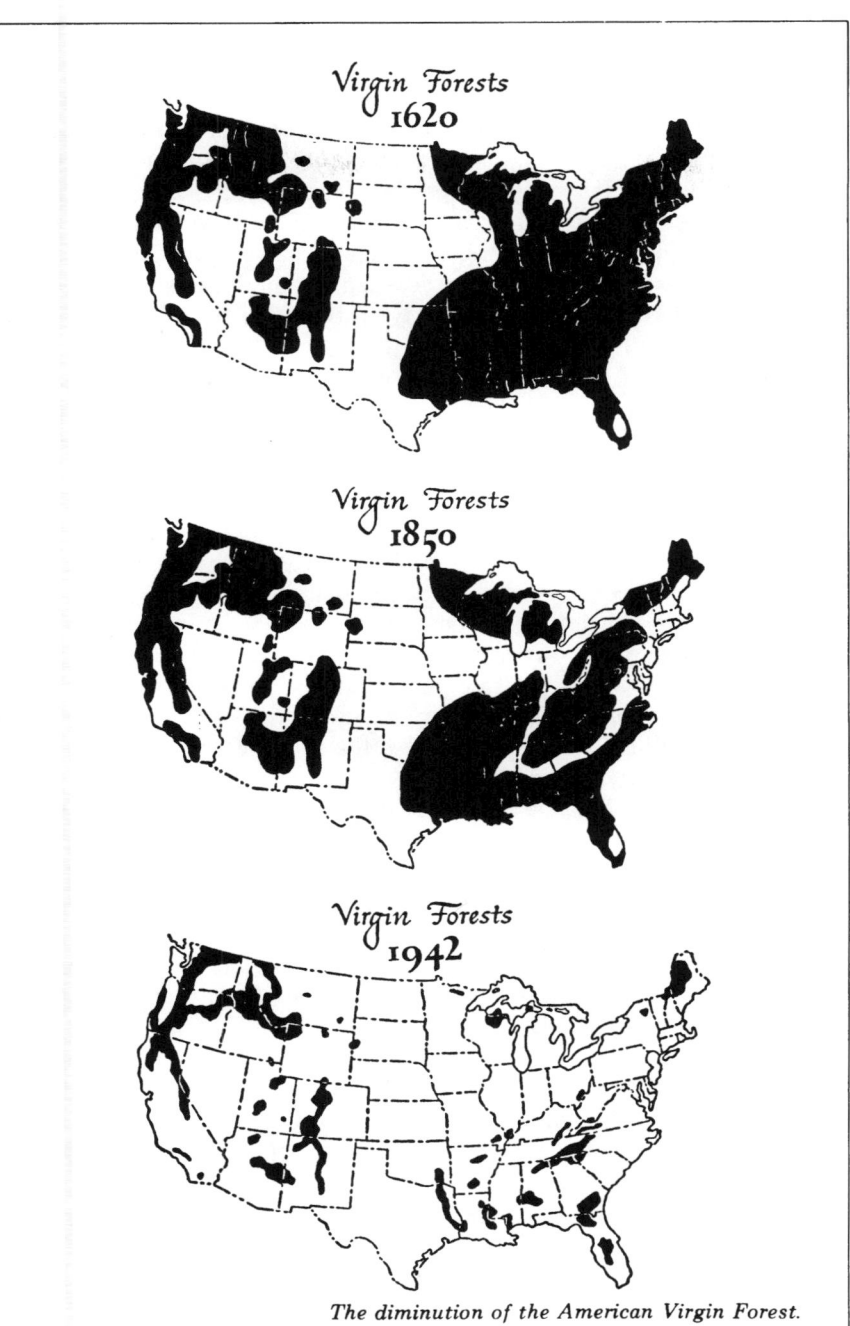

Virgin Forests
1620

Virgin Forests
1850

Virgin Forests
1942

The diminution of the American Virgin Forest.

which sparked a new conservation crusade. Forests took on a whole new aspect, no longer viewed solely as a source of material supply but as a place in which man's body and mind could secure renewal. Forest recreation was given a high priority in the Forest Service's Multiple Use Act of 1960. The public took a much more critical attitude toward the management of its forests. Open confrontations occurred, such as when the Forest Service proposed in the 1960's to establish a giant recreational area at Mount Rogers in the Jefferson National Forest. Environmentalists adamantly opposed and finally defeated the proposal on the ground that it would greatly impair the quality of life and devastate a unique forest resource.

As a result of these changing attitudes and changing public pressures, the southern national forests, such as Pisgah, George Washington, and the Cherokee, came under multiple use management, with environmental protection and outdoor recreation taking their place alongside timber, watershed, and wildlife management. The significance of this changing use is illustrated by 1983 visitor use just in the Pisgah National Forest: 494,300 hikers utilized the forest, as did 851,600 campers, 914,800 sightseers, and 536,000 hunters.

To help cope with this increased demand and to relieve an ever-present unemployment, a conservation program similar to the CCC was instituted, the Job Corps, with camps scattered all over the nation. In addition, Youth Conservation Corps and Young Adult Conservation Corps were established—all aimed at relieving unemployment and improving natural resources.

But one of the most remarkable changes in the use of the forest has been the advent of wilderness designation and use. Originally "wilderness" meant a cursed land to which undesirables were banished. Today more and more people are preaching Thoreau's philosophy: "In wildness is the preservation of the world." And since less than two percent of the nation's original wilderness still exits, Congress in 1964 set aside select lands as "Wilderness Areas," places for man to visit for personal, soul revival.

Along with the recreational and wilderness uses, the traditional usage of the Appalachian forests continue. They are still producing lumber, pulpwood, fuel, and all the other resources man finds so useful from the forests. Indeed, they are well fulfilling the purpose which Gifford Pinchot, this nation's first career forester, stipulated they should fulfill: "The rightful use and purpose of our natural resources is to make all the people strong and well, able and wise, well taught, well fed, well clothed, and well housed, full of knowledge and initiative, with equal opportunity for all and special privileges for none."

To see the fantastic variety of forests and their use in Southern

Appalachia, one might take a short ride on the Blue Ridge Parkway from Mount Mitchell to the Great Smokies National Park. In the process, one would encounter Mount Mitchell's state park forests, then the Parkway's federal park forests, the United States Forest Service at Bent Creek, the Pisgah and Natahala National Forests, the forests of many small private owners, the commercial forests of Champion Paper Company, the forest of the Cherokee Indians, and finally the national park forests of the Great Smoky Mountains National Park. All of these are practicing forests, all with a different function, but all part of our rendezvous with the land.

Harley E. Jolley
Mars Hill College

EPILOGUE

As the great Forest in the Southern Appalachians diminished in time and space, it grew ever larger as an IDEA. It is the IDEA of the Forest that commands our attention today. It is the idea of the Forest; its original grandeur and its profound affect on our history that engenders so many voices and so many uses. Almost every one of us holds and nurtures some part of that idea. Collectively, we may recall and represent all the meanings of the Forest over 10,000 years of human minds and history: the hunter, the gatherer, the reaper, the sower, the walker, the dreamer, the seeker, the hider, the mother, the child, the in-dweller, the stranger, the singer, the winged, the four-legged, the two-legged, the lost and those who have come home, from father to son, all have some notion, some emotion in response to this incomprehensible wilderness and beauty which now by our own hand is gone but cannot, will not, ever leave us.

S.G.

Photographs courtesy of U.S. Forest Service.
Photographs page 7 courtesy of Cherokee Historical Association.

SUGGESTED READINGS

Ayers, H. B., and Ashe, W. W. *The Southern Appalachian Forests*. Washington: U. S. Geological Survey, Professional Paper 37, 1905.

Bakeless, John C. *Daniel Boone, Master of the Wilderness*. New York, William Morrow & Co., 1939.

Bingham, Edgar. "Appalachia: Underdeveloped, Overdeveloped, or Wrongly Developed?" *The Virginia Geographer*, *VII* (Winter, 1972), 9-12.

Bingham, Edgar. "The Impact of Recreational Development on Pioneer Lifestyles in Southern Appalachia." *Proceedings of the Pioneer America Society*, (1973), 59-69.

Campbell, Carlos C. *Birth of a National Park in the Great Smoky Mountains*. Knoxville: University of Tennessee Press, 1969.

Campbell, John C. *The Southern Highlander and His Homeland*. New York: The Russell Sage Foundation, 1921.

Caudill, Harry. *Night Comes to the Cumberlands*. Boston: Little, Brown and Company, 1962.

Cronon, William. *Changes in the Land: Indians, Colonists, and the Ecology of New England*. New York: Hilland Wang, 1983.

Day, G. M. "The Indian as an Ecological Factor in the Northeastern Forest." *Ecology*, 34 (1953), 329-46.

Dickens, Roy S., Jr. *Cherokee Prehistory, The Pisgah Phase in the Appalachian Summit Region*. Knoxville: The University of Tennessee Press, 1976.

Eller, Ronald D. "Land and Family: A Historical View of Preindustrial Appalachia." *Appalachian Journal*, 6 (Winter, 1979), 83-111.

Eller, Ronald D. *Miners, Millhands, and Mountaineers: Industrialization of the Appalachian South, 1880-1930*. Knoxville: The University of Tennessee Press, 1982.

Ford, Thomas R., ed. *The Southern Appalachian Region: A Survey*. Lexington University of Kentucky Press, 1962.

Frome, Michael. *Battle for the Wilderness*. New York: Praeger Publishers, 1974.

Gilbert, W. H. *The Eastern Cherokee*. Washington: Smithsonian Institution, 1943.

Huth, Hans. *Nature and the American: Three Centuries of Changing Attitudes*. Lincoln: University of Nebraska Press, 1957.

Hudson, Charles. *The Southeastern Indians*. Knoxville: University of Tennessee Press, 1976.

Jolley, Harley E. "The Cradle of Forestry: Where Tree Power Started." *American Forests*, 76 (October, November, December, 1970).

Kahn, Si. *The Forest Service and Appalachia*. New York: The John Hay Whitney Foundation, 1974.

Kephart, Horace. *Our Southern Highlands*. New York, 1913; rpt. Knoxville: University of Tennessee Press, 1976.

King, Duane H., ed. *The Cherokee Indian Nation*. Knoxville: The University of Tennessee Press, 1979.

Mastran, Shelley Smith and Lowerre, Nan. *Mountaineers and Rangers: A History of Federal Forest Management in the Southern Appalachians, 1900-81*. Washington: United States Department of Agriculture, 1983.

McDonald, Forest and McWhiney, Grady. "The South from Self-Sufficiency to Peonage: An Interpretation." *American Historical Review,* 85 (December 1980), 1095-1118.

Michaux, F. A. *Travels to the Westward of the Alleghany Mountains in the States of the Ohio, Kentucky and Tennessee in the Year 1802.* London: Barnard and Sultzer, 1805.

Nash, Roderick. "The American Cult of the Primitive." *American Quarterly,* 18 (Fall, 1966), 518-537.

Nash, Roderick, ed. *The Call of the Wild.* New York: George Brogiller, 1970.

Nesbitt, W. A. "History of Early Settlement and Land Use on the Bent Creek Experimental Forest, Buncombe County, N. C." Unpublished report, Southeastern Forest Experimental Station, 1941.

Pinchot, Gifford. *Breaking New Ground.* New York, 1947; rpt. Seattle: University of Washington Press, 1972.

Pomeroy, Kenneth B. and Yoho, James G. *North Carolina Lands: Ownership, Use and Management of Forest and Related Lands.* Washington: The American Forestry Association, 1964.

Robinson, Glen O. *The Forest Service: A Study in Public Land Management.* Baltimore: The Johns Hopkins University Press, 1975.

Rothrock, Mary U., ed. *The French Broad-Holston Country.* Knoxville, 1946; rpt. Knoxville: East Tennessee Historical Society, 1972.

Schmitt, Peter J. *Back to Nature: The Arcadian Myth in Urban America.* New York: Oxford University Press, 1969.

Shands, William E. and Healy, Robert G. *The Lands Nobody Wanted.* Washington: The Conservation Foundation, 1977.

Shapiro, Henry D. *Appalachia On Our Mind: The Southern Mountains and Mountaineers in the American Consciousness, 1870-1920.* Chapel Hill: University of North Carolina Press, 1978.

Swanton, John R. *The Indians of the Southeastern United States.* Washington, DC: Smithsonian Institution Press, 1979.

Thompson, D. Q., and Smith, R. "The Forest Primeval in the Northeast—A Great Myth?" Paper presented at the Tall Timbers Fires Ecology Conference, 1970.

Truett, Randle Bond. *Trade and Travel Around the Southern Appalachians Before 1830.* Chapel Hill: University of North Carolina Press, 1935.

Turner, Frederick Jackson. *Rise of the New West, 1819-1829.* New York: Collier Books, 1962.

Turner, Frederick Jackson. "The Significance of the Frontier in American History" in *The Frontier in American History.* New York: Henry Holt and Co., 1920.

Van Noppen, John and Van Noppen, Ina. *Western North Carolina Since the Civil War.* Boone, N. C.: Appalachian Consortium Press, 1975.

Weller, Jack E. *Yesterday's People: Life in Contemporary Appalachia.* Lexington: University of Kentucky Press, 1965.

Williamson, J. W., ed. *An Appalachan Symposium: Essays Written in Honor of Cratis D. Williams.* Boone, N. C.: Appalachian State University Press, 1977.

ABOUT THE AUTHOR

BARRY M. BUXTON has been a teacher, researcher, publisher, editor, and community leader with extensive international experience. He received his Ph.D. from the University of Nebraska. Currently Buxton serves as the president of Lees-McRae College. Prior to his tenure at Lees-McRae, he served as the Vice President of Special Projects at the Savannah College of Art and Design. Buxton has also served as president of various science and history museums in North Carolina, Texas, and Georgia. During the 1980s, he served as Executive Director of the sixteen-member Appalachian Consortium Press.

Made in United States
Orlando, FL
22 March 2026